Conversations with
EUGENE
IONESCO

Conversations with Eugene Ionesco

Claude Bonnefoy

Translated by Jan Dawson

HOLT, RINEHART AND WINSTON
New York   Chicago   San Francisco

CONTENTS

Discovery

Claude Bonnefoy. Eugène Ionesco, you appeared on the French scene in 1950 when your first play, *The Bald Prima Donna*, was produced at the Noctambules by Nicolas Bataille. This play was so disconcerting and broke so completely with everything the public was used to that it stirred up violent reactions—some enthusiastic, some plain contemptuous. Today, even if there are still some people who refuse to understand—or to recognize their own insignificance in the way the Smiths and Martins talk and act—*The Bald Prima Donna* has become a classic of the new theatre. You are now a famous author, and your plays are not only performed but studied and discussed throughout the world.

But a playwright's existence doesn't begin with his first work. This first play implies a good deal of preliminary thought about the theatre, about life and literature, and is likely to have been preceded by other attempts. A work doesn't exist autonomously: it grows out of a personality, a human life—in other words, an accumulation of events, emotions, passions and dreams.

Before we start to talk about your plays—about your dramatic theories, your favourite themes and, possibly, about your reaction to the way certain critics have interpreted them—I should like us to go back into your past and ferret out some of the events, ideas, feelings and discoveries that have been important to you. The way

9

the Inspector makes Choubert go back in *Victims of Duty*. But don't worry. I shan't be as cruel as your Inspector. I just want to trace the emotions and ideas that led to your becoming a writer. And to do this, I think we should take things chronologically. At the end of *The Colonel's Photograph*, you published *Spring 1939*, a fragment of a diary in which you evoke your childhood. Now, since your plays are extremely oneiric, is it fair to assume that some of the dreams contained in them are your own childhood dreams?

Eugène Ionesco. Childhood dreams? No. I have childhood memories—pictures, lights and colours. But no dreams. If dreams often provide the material for my plays, the fact that I can recall them so precisely means that they must be fairly recent ones. I attach great importance to dreams because they give me a sharper, more penetrating vision of myself. Dreaming is thinking. But much deeper, truer, more authentic than ordinary thinking, because one is somehow forced inside oneself. A dream is a kind of meditation, of communion with oneself. A thought in pictures. Sometimes it can be extremely revealing, and extremely cruel. It has an absolutely luminous and inescapable clarity.

For the playwright, a dream can be considered as an essentially dramatic event. The dream is pure drama. In a dream, one is always in mid-situation. To be more concise, I think that the dream is a lucid thought, more lucid than any one has when awake, a thought expressed in images, and that at the same time its form is always dramatic. A dream is always dramatic because in a dream one is always in mid-situation. But we can go into all this later on.

C.B. Could you tell me about some of these childhood memories and images? Which particular emotions have left a lasting mark on you?

E.I. My mother's sadness; the revelation of death; and loneliness, my mother's loneliness: these are the negative side of my childhood. But there was also the country, the days at La Chapelle-Anthenaise, days of fullness, happiness and sunlight.

C.B. What was this experience of loneliness?

E.I. Not loneliness. My mother's loneliness. It's hard to explain. My father had had to go back to Bucharest, and I could see my mother, miserable and alone, struggling to earn enough money, struggling against all the cruelty around her, a bit like Josephine in *A Stroll in the Air*.

C.B. And the revelation of death?

E.I. I've already written about what I felt whenever I saw a funeral—those long processions filing past right under the windows of the house where I lived; and how I'd ask my mother what it meant. 'Someone is dead.' 'Why? Why is he dead?' 'He's dead because he was ill.' As I finally understood it, people died because they'd been ill, because they'd had an accident—whatever happened, death was an accident—and if you took great care not to be ill, if you were very good, if you always wore your muffler and took your medicine, if you looked both ways before you crossed the street, then you wouldn't ever have to die. It bothered me, particularly because I had noticed that people grew older. I wondered, 'How long can you go on growing old? Just how far can you go?' I would imagine a man ageing—I would see him growing taller, then I'd see him growing bent. I'd see his beard start to grow white, then get whiter and whiter and longer and longer; it would be trailing behind him and he would be getting more and more bent all the time. And I'd say to myself: 'No. It's not possible. It has to end somewhere.' One day I asked my mother. 'We're all going to die, aren't we? Tell me the truth.' She said,

'Yes.' I must have been four years old, maybe five; I was sitting on the ground and she was standing over me. I can still see her. She had her hands clasped behind her back. She was leaning against the wall. When she saw me sobbing—because suddenly I had begun to cry—she just looked at me in a sad, helpless way. I was very frightened. I kept thinking that she was certainly going to die one day. And I couldn't stop thinking about it. . . . Perhaps I was not so much afraid of death as of her death. But the odd thing is, the way all these impressions, all this anguish, disappeared once I got into the country, where I lived for three years, far away from my mother who was, possibly, the unconscious cause of my anguish.

C.B.   And did this anguish later return?

E.I.   It did, it still torments me. It returned—I can't remember the exact moment—after I got back from La Chapelle-Anthenaise. It returned because I had discovered time: Sundays and Thursdays[1] that were inevitably followed by Mondays. Even the longest holiday had to come to an end, and every moment of pleasure had at its centre a kind of hole that was slowly sucking it all in; every hour would be thrown into the past. At La Chapelle-Anthenaise, time didn't exist. I just lived in the present. And living was a joy, a state of grace.

C.B.   How old were you?

E.I.   Eight, nine. Perhaps ten.

C.B.   And what does this country experience represent for you?

E.I.   A kind of completeness. A symbolization, if you'll forgive the word, of paradise. La Chapelle-Anthenaise is still for me the image of a paradise lost. I left it to go to

[1] NOTE: Thursday is a school holiday in France.

12

Paris, then to Rumania. It grew further away both in time and in space.

C.B. Why was it a paradise?

E.I. Why? . . . Why? . . . Why? . . . It was as if things were going away and coming back, and I wasn't moving at all. Spring would go away, with its sky and its flowers. It would go away and be replaced by summer, then by winter that brought me other colours, other landscapes; and then it would come back. The world was turning round me. Time was a wheel that was spinning round me, while I remained immovable and eternal. I was the centre of the world. And then, alas, a centrifugal force pushed me into the circle, into time. I was living in a very beautiful, very old house. It wasn't a château, it was an old farmhouse called 'The Mill'. In fact it was an old mill that hadn't been used for a hundred years. . . . This house was in an extraordinary spot, at the intersection of three or four paths and surrounded by tiny hills and bushes. It was a nest, a natural shelter. In that house—it was rather dark, the way all country houses were in those days—I had an extraordinary feeling of comfort. Everything seemed to be a kind of symbol. As we were living at the bottom of the little valley, we had to climb up a slight slope that was known as 'the pug dog' to get to the nearest small town. What you noticed particularly as you climbed 'the pug dog' was the church steeple. I remember one very happy, very sunny morning when I was going to church in my Sunday clothes. I can still see the blue sky and, in the sky, the spire of the church. I can still hear the bells. There was heaven. There was the earth. It was the perfect marriage of heaven and earth. I believe certain psychoanalysts, the Jungians, say that we suffer because we experience within ourselves the separation of heaven and earth. But in that valley there was a true marriage of earth and heaven.

It's only now that I'm trying to explain why I felt so happy there. At that time, I was living in my paradise. I didn't need to explain it. There were the colours, vivid colours, fresher and more intense than they'll ever be again. My favourite colours, especially a pure, virgin blue. There were the primroses in springtime, and the opening up of the path. That too was a mystery. That too had a profound meaning, an elementary truth. In winter, the path was muddy, literally closed. You couldn't walk along it. Then, suddenly, the landscape was somehow transfigured. Everything became filled with life—flowers and squirrels and birds in song and golden insects. I felt it really was the resurrection of a dead world—the world of mud and petrified trees whose arms were now stretching out and coming back to life.

C.B. So essentially, what counted for you was this feeling of being in harmony with the natural rhythms?

E.I. Yes, and the certainty of this resurrection. There was something else as well. There was freedom. When I came to Paris, later, at about the age of eleven, I was very unhappy. It seemed like a prison. The streets of Paris were the prison and the large houses the prison walls.

C.B. Wasn't freedom, in the country, the same thing as space?

E.I. The country was both space and nest at the same time.

C.B. In *Spring 1939*, you say that you went to school with the village children. Did you feel that school at La Chapelle-Anthenaise was different from school in Paris?

E.I. Oh yes!

C.B. Yet the lessons were the same.

E.I. Yes, but the school in the village wasn't a barracks. It was a tiny little house. The village was a tiny village, with just a few hundred inhabitants. In the boys' school, there were forty-five or fifty of us. There was only one classroom, with three sections in it; the master would spend some time with one section, then go on to another. Everything was smaller, on a more human scale. The village was a cosmos, both space and nest at the same time, both solitude (which we all need) and community. It was not a limited world, it was a complete one.

C.B. Complete *and* familiar?

E.I. Everyone, and everything, had a face. Religion had a face, the priest's face. Authority had a face, the mayor's, or the local policeman's. Knowledge had a face, the schoolmaster's. Labour had a face, the blacksmith's. Everything was personalized, concrete.

C.B. But weren't you then tempted to project on to the institutions or the values they represented the feelings you had about the priest, the policeman, the schoolmaster, etc.?

E.I. No. Their function was visible and concrete, but we had no difficulty in distinguishing between the function and the person. For instance, we had no difficulty in distinguishing between the function of the priest and the priest himself, a drunkard whom everyone laughed at. This didn't stop us believing in his religion or going to church or learning our catechism. It was the same with the schoolmaster. The schoolmaster was Monsieur Guéné: he had his worries and his family troubles and at the same time he taught us to read and write, taught us history and geography, including the history of Mayenne, because in those days you were taught regional

15

history as well. In other words, they were all just people who had divided up the different functions amongst themselves. The unpleasant thing about society nowadays, is that there's a confusion between people and their functions; or rather, people are tempted to identify completely with the function they perform: instead of a function taking on a human face, you get a man dehumanising himself, losing his face. This is what's happening, particularly in totalitarian societies. I've often thought that what is really upsetting, dehumanizing, is the fact that an official sleeps with his uniform on. He's an official, totally, metaphysically. It's probably because 'functions' have become so important that there's so much talk about sociology right now. It suggests a definite alienation. A man ought not to be absorbed to a total, totalitarian degree by his social function. We know that man has never been as alienated as he is now, particularly in the socialist societies where there is so much talk about dis-alienating him. Of course, man was alienated before, but not to such an extent. But in the village, a man wasn't confused with his function. Father Durand was *acting* the priest, old Father So-and-So was *acting* the policeman, like actors playing their parts, whereas today a 'man of letters' is a 'man of letters' even in his dreams, or almost; he has a 'man of letters' tie, a 'man of letters' wife and 'man os letters' friends, he's abolished by his function, he if nothing more than his alienating function, he's no longer anything. He's swallowed up by the social machinery. And the social machinery is society turned monster, turned ogre.

C.B. Do you feel that your plays owe something to your memories of La Chapelle-Anthenaise?

E.I. Yes, a lot of my preoccupations and obsessions come from La Chapelle-Anthenaise, and also from my being forced to leave my paradise.

Everything we live through leaves some mark on us.

Yes, I was a child, a little man in his own reality . . . a schoolboy from time to time, but not essentially a schoolboy . . . a child who, among other things, went to school . . . not a cog in a machine. . . . In other words, not a creature with a single, impoverishing function that robs man of one of his dimensions.

Claude Bonnefoy. You say in *Notes and Counter-Notes*, 'It was chance that formed us', and you also say that if we had not had the same teachers, not met the same people or lived through the same events, we would be different, we would think differently. It's obvious, after what you've told me, that your experience of the country, when you were a child, played an important part in forming your sensibility. And when we come to talk about your plays, we shall find these same themes: the nest, the lost paradise, the theme of colour, the opposition between man and his function, between the individual and the social mechanism.

For the moment, I should like to come back to the idea of chance, to those random factors which give each man's years of apprenticeship their unique quality. Were there in fact in your childhood, in your youth, any people, any teachers or friends, any events that had a profound or lasting influence on you?

Eugène Ionesco. I'd forgotten that sentence about our being formed by chance. I'm no longer sure that it's true. I don't know if I still believe in chance. I wonder if we don't make what we ourselves want of the things that happen to us, of the teachers that we get. It's true the events and the teachers we get are a matter of chance, but we ourselves do something with this chance in our own particular way. Of course I was influenced by my university teachers in Rumania. But I was often influenced in a very odd way: contrarily. I didn't think the same way as they did. I may just be obstreperous, just naturally contrary. In any case, I wasn't receptive to them. My constant attitude, my natural tendency, my inclination was to fight them.

For instance, I had a teacher of 'literary aesthetics' whose ambition was to work out a precise way of measuring poetry. We all know that criticism seems impossible, that criteria vary, that critical criteria don't touch the heart of the work, that, when they talk about a literary work, what critics are really doing is discussing it as psychology or sociology or history or literary history and so on. In other words, they're always off to one side of the work, in the context; the text hardly concerns them at all, although it's the most important thing; it's the text one has to see, in other words the uniqueness of the work, which is a living organism, a creation with living creatures inside it;[1] not the context, by which I mean the general aspects, the external or impersonal aspects. What matters to me in any particular work is not what it has in common with other works, but what makes it unlike any other: not its sociology or its history but its irreducible existence in history and in society—this particular story, the story of this book and not of any other. What that teacher wanted to find was a criterion that was both relevant and very precise. He wanted to measure exactly, quantitively, the specific quality, the value of each work—as a project it was some kind of

[1] NOTE: There is no exact translation for the phrase *créature créaturée* that Ionesco employs here.

quest for the absolute, but it was a bit crude as well. He said there were works of skill, works of talent, and works of genius. He wanted to be able to measure the relative quantities of skill, talent and genius in any work. He wanted to be able to weigh them. It was a very interesting project, and now that I come to think of it, it seems to me that someone ought to try it again, just because it *is* an impossible undertaking.

In those days I was against him, quite simply because I had a tendency to define myself in opposition to someone else. He would defend his system; I'd counter by bringing up Croce, whom I was reading at the time.

At other times, the differences between me and my teachers went much deeper, and I don't think they were just an expression of adolescent revolt. I'm thinking particularly of some of the teachers at Bucharest who had then become Nazified; theorists of Racism, Nietzscheans or sub-Nietzscheans, emulators of Rosenberg—or even of Spengler (who was not in favour with the Nazis but who was a pre-Nazifier just the same).

C.B. But wasn't there more than simple revolt in your opposition to your aesthetics teacher? Wasn't it because you wanted to write, or because you had already written, that you revolted against an attempt to reduce a literary work to a set of figures?

E.I. Perhaps. Only my ideas weren't very clear at the age of eighteen. At that time I was extremely influenced— particularly when I was trying my hand for a while at literary criticism—not by my teacher, whose name was Dragomiresco, but by Croce. In any case, one of Croce's ideas has stayed with me: namely that you can't really distinguish between quality and originality, in other words, that the whole history of art is the history of its expression. Every time there's a new form of expression, it's an event, something happens, something new. That's what has stayed with me: expression is both style and content. Every work is like a child, born of its parents, yet different from its parents, both irreplaceable and unique. Every individual is unique. Every work is an individual, a separate being. A work is unique, or, in other words, great when it's original, unexpected and at the same time a culmination of history; both what has produced it and something else as well. I've also retained from Croce the idea that there are two kinds of thought: discursive thought and intuitive thought. Or to put it differently, logical thought and aesthetic thought. For this reason, really, I think that dreams are the pure expression of intuitive thought, they *are* aesthetic thought. Dreams are thoughts directly formulated in images. For all my resistance, I still have something of my aesthetics teacher in me, the ambition, the need to find definitive and precise criteria—although I know that, for literature, it's an impossible task. There are certain things I continue to believe, because of that teacher and others. In particular, that criticism is not a matter of psychology, or politics, but that there must be a system of criticism appropriate to each work. But which? I think we have to judge according to the laws, to the rules, that each new work imposes on us. Is it consistent with its own goals? It seems odd, paradoxical, that it should contain its own criteria within itself. Though what exactly does 'its own criteria' mean? We'll have to try and get to the bottom of all this. Perhaps the best ways of approach are through psychology, sociology and literary history . . . it's when these means want not just to approach the work, but to absorb it ideologically or sociologically or dogmatically that there's something wrong.

C.B.   Wouldn't the essential thing be to start by analysing structures?

E.I.   Of course.

C.B. You've just spoken about your Rumanian teachers. Did the fact that you had from the start a double culture, French and Rumanian, give you something extra, or was it on the contrary the cause, if not of a deep anguish, then at least of a few tensions?

E.I. The situation did result in tensions: but the anguish was sometimes a good thing. I arrived in Bucharest when I was thirteen years old and I didn't come back till I was twenty-six. I learnt Rumanian there. When I was fourteen, fifteen, I had bad marks in Rumanian. At seventeen or eighteen, I had good marks in Rumanian. I had learned to write. I wrote my first poems in Rumanian. I no longer wrote as well in French. I made mistakes. When I came back to France, I still knew French, of course, but I no longer knew how to write it. I mean write in the 'literary' sense. I had to get used to it again. This learning and unlearning and relearning were, I think, interesting exercises.

And also, yes, there was an anguish, because in Rumania I felt I was in exile.

C.B. Do you remember any events or emotions which, like your childhood experience at La Chapelle-Anthenaise, were of importance to you later on?

E.I. Yes . . . an officer in the street slapping a peasant or a poor man across the face because he wouldn't salute or had forgotten to salute the flag. Students beating up people whose noses weren't very orthodox. Yes, memories of violence, of bourgeois stupidity, of captains and officers walking in the streets showing off their well-polished boots, of military service, in other words of odious or disagreeable things. All the same, I did have friends. We'll talk about them some other time, perhaps. And I also met my wife there.

C.B. So there was at least one happy event?

E.I.   I think that life with my wife is a rich, an important thing. It's something that never stops growing. Don't you find that the important events, the pleasant or unpleasant or unexpected events are most often of the simple, everyday kind? I could write about it indefinitely, whole volumes.

C.B.   Let's get back to your life in Bucharest.

E.I.   In spite of everything, what was really interesting about it was precisely these violent conflicts with a milieu in which I felt ill at ease—this conflict, not with ideas but with feelings that I couldn't accept. Because really, before becoming ideological, Nazism, Fascism, etc. start out as feelings. All ideologies, including Marxism, are simply justifications and alibis for certain feelings, certain passions, and for more or less biological instincts. Later on, the conflict became more serious. I had made a certain number of friends. And a lot of them—I'm talking about 1932, 1933, 1934, 1935—turned to Fascism. Just as today all the intellectuals are 'progressivists', as they call themselves, because it's fashionable. At that time, it was fashionable to be on the right. In France too, it was the same thing, with Drieu La Rochelle, the *Camelots du Roi*,[1] etc. . . . I don't like the 'progressivist' clichés any more than I liked the Fascist clichés and it seems to me that today's progressivists are a bit like yesterday's Fascists. There's some truth in it—it's the children of the old Fascists who are 'progressivist' nowadays. In France, social rebels are always recruited amongst the 'intellectual' middle classes . . . one revolt behind the times. Keeping up with the times is the same as being behind them: you need to keep one step ahead of them.

In Bucharest the rift was there. I felt more and more alone. There were a certain number of us who didn't

[1] NOTE: *Les Camelots du Roi* was the name of the *Action Française* youth group.

22

want to accept the slogans and the ideologies that were thrust at us. It was very difficult to resist, I don't mean just on the level of political action (which would obviously have been very difficult) but also on the simple level of a moral and intellectual resistance, even a silent resistance, because when you're twenty years old and you have teachers who offer you scientific or pseudo-scientific theories and explanations, when you have newspapers, when you have a whole atmosphere, doctrines, a whole movement against you, it's really very hard to resist, hard not to let yourself be convinced; luckily, my wife helped me a great deal.

C.B. That sounds just like the story of Bérenger in *Rhinoceros*.

E.I. Exactly. I've always been suspicious of collective truths. I think an idea is true when it hasn't been put into words and that the moment it's put into words it becomes exaggerated. Because the moment it's put into words there's an abuse, an excess in the expression of the idea that makes it false. It's possible that I may hold the idea I've just put to you because of another great thinker whom I've met a few times and read more often: Emmanuel Mounier. Mounier constantly made that extraordinary effort of lucidity which consists of seeing what's true and what's false in every historical utterance. He was the only person to make this effort of lucidity, this effort to separate the true from the false. Nowadays, it's not done any more. People are carried away by their passions, they refuse to elucidate them because they want to hold on to them. The more important people are, the more they're carried away by their passions and the more they add to the sum of confusion and chaos. Look at Sartre.

C.B. I'm sure we'll get the chance to talk about Sartre later. But I should like to ask you one last question about

Rumania. Do you think you owe anything to Rumanian literature?

E.I.   There are some very interesting Rumanian writers, a great dramatist called Caragiale, but Caragiale was himself influenced by the authors who influenced me too, by the Flaubert of the *Idées Recues*,[1] by Henri Monnier, by Labiche, There was another writer, an absurdist writer, a pre-surrealist whom I liked a lot called Urmuz; and he owed a lot to Jarry. In other words, there is no Rumanian literature that really influenced me. Of course, I might have been affected by other Rumanian writers. There were the anonymous folk poets—there's a lot of very fine Rumanian folk poetry. But the themes of the great anonymous poets were not my themes. Basically, they didn't concern me.

C.B.   So you *do* owe something to the years you spent in Rumania as an adolescent and as a young man: first, because of your teachers, even if it was in reaction against them and also because of your first critical essays, some definite ideas about literary aesthetics; then, an experience of life: your feelings of exile, your conflicts with various ideologies, the discovery of love. All this—all these experiences, good or bad—contributed to your formation as a man and a writer. But the discovery of literature, and of the theatre, must have come from somewhere else.

---

[1] NOTE: English translations have appeared under two titles: *Dictionary of Accepted Ideas*; *Dictionary of Platitudes.*

Claude Bonnefoy. What were the first books that really affected you, that perhaps gave you the incentive to write?

Eugène Ionesco. There were lots of them, and they kept changing. As a child, like all children, I used to read fairy stories; next I read the life of Turenne, the life of Condé. Later still, I liked very old stories. At La Chapelle-Anthenaise, all the popular literature of the eighteenth century.

C.B.   Penny dreadfuls, you mean?

E.I.   Yes. In those days people were still reading them. For instance, there was the story of a child who's taking his first communion and bites into the host. And his mouth fills with blood. The blood of the Lord. Or else his mouth catches on fire, he's burned because he bit into the host. There were also ghost stories, stories about werewolves and pilgrims. But none of this can have had any influence on me. It's all very remote. In any case, I know that I discovered literature through Flaubert, a little later, when I was eleven or twelve. Reading *A Simple Heart*, I had the sudden revelation of literary beauty, of literary quality, of style. Of course, I'd already read *Les Misérables*, but I hadn't received the same shock. Before this, it seems to me, I used to read everything, including some of the classics—I'd read one or two novels by Balzac, some other novels by Hugo, *The Three Musketeers*—and also comics like *Le Cricri* and *L'Epatant*, and detective stories. But after I discovered *A Simple Heart*, I found it impossible to read bad novelettes or cheap detective stories.

There are some people who have a feeling for literature the way other people have an ear for music. I think I had a feeling for literature. My school friends went on reading inferior quality books. They didn't realize the difference between good and bad; what interested them, as far as I could make out, was the story, what happened to the characters, what they did. But I couldn't go on reading the stories they read because they were badly written. I had understood literature, understood that it's not the story that counts, but above all how it is written; in other words, that any story should reveal a deeper meaning. To care more about *how* a story is told than about *what* it tells is the true sign of a literary vocation.

C.B.   After you discovered *A Simple Heart*, did you attempt to read all of Flaubert?

E.I.   No, I was still too young to persevere methodically at anything. However, discovering Flaubert didn't prevent me, later on, from admiring some minor poets.

C.B.   For instance?

E.I.   Albert Samain, Francis Jammes, Maeterlinck. They were still writing at the time. And they knew how to write. Unfortunately, they were a little silly. When I re-read them now, I can see I was mistaken.

C.B.   But wasn't there in Samain, Jammes and Maeterlinck a taste for reverie that attracted you, something that satisfied the ambiguous aspirations of any adolescent?

E.I.   Yes, of course, that was it. These poets all expressed something vague and uncertain. They had a disastrous influence on me, because they instilled in me a sentimentality that at times I still find hard to shake off. Originally, they corresponded to the adolescent temperament, to my own temperament. Later, fortunately, I discovered Flaubert. But more than the Flaubert of *Madame Bovary* I loved, and still love, the Flaubert of *Sentimental Education*. It is his most complete book. There is in it a satire of second-hand ideas, of clichés whose intellectual poverty makes them dangerous; and

there is style. There is love, there is a feeling of time un-
ravelling, there is the 1848 revolution seen with a
critical eye. So: imaginary, historical and critical at the
same time; it is *the* work of art, *the* novel *par excellence*, a
whole world, complex and complete.

There's one author to whom I've never really re-
sponded. At that time, everybody was reading and enjoying Gide's *Fruits of the Earth*. I couldn't stand it, because
of the rhetoric. Everybody said it was a well-written
book, I found it badly written, sentimental, false and
pretentious.

C.B. At that time, what did you look for in a literary work?

E.I. The first thing I liked about *A Simple Heart* was a kind of
luminousness, a kind of light inside the words. I felt the
same thing later when I was reading something by
Charles du Bos, a book of literary criticism, I can't
remember which one; his criticism was rather ordinary,
but he had a style—what, in my private language, I call
a luminous style. I also found it in Valéry Larbaud, in
that story about the lesbian lovers. They are in a house
with slatted blinds, and the image of that shadow and
light in the room is something that's never left me. And
I liked as much, or even more, Valéry Larbaud's *Enfan-
tines*, that really luminous text that evoked my own
vision of childhood.

C.B. What other writers have given you this impression of
light?

E.I. Alain-Fournier, who inspired my adolescent dreams and
writings. In my mind, when they talked about Fournier's
father's house, I saw the setting for *Le Grand Meaulnes* as
La Chapelle-Anthenaise, I could see the story taking
place there. The images from my childhood would enfold the images from Alain-Fournier and I would see the
landscapes, know the place where the lost path was. I

could see that lost path very clearly in the grounds of the village château.

Valéry Larbaud, du Bos, Alain-Fournier, Flaubert—I loved these authors because in their books there was something that went beyond the text, that wasn't contained in it, things that perhaps were more in me. In all of them I felt this same presence of light. Then too, among the books that have influenced me most, that spoke to me of light, there are the ones by the Byzantines of the twelfth, thirteenth and fourteenth centuries, the Hesychasts, and there's also an Arseniev book *The Russian Church* which tells how a man who's unhappy, tormented and sick comes to a priest, a monk; and when the monk places his hand on his shoulder, the sick man feels a great happiness, a fullness, everything in the world becomes radiant, he's enveloped in a great light and he's cured.

Really, I don't know what this light corresponds to. Obviously one mustn't immediately give it a mystical significance, but I should like to know its psychological significance, to know why I need it, to know why, every time I have a feeling of light, I become happy.

Claude Bonnefoy. We started out trying to define your literary tastes, to establish the authors who were important for you and who perhaps had a more or less direct influence on your work. But since our discussions about literature have led to this theme of light which occurs as frequently in your plays and stories as its opposite, the theme of mud and engulfing slime—and, on the social level, of alienation—we might at this point open a parenthesis and try to discover what were for you the literary or non-literary sources of these themes; what for you were or are their concrete manifestations. It will help us later on to understand both your own imagination and the meaning of your work. This is why I shall begin by asking if, leaving aside the books you've mentioned, you personally have ever been overwhelmed by a sense of light.

Eugène Ionesco. Yes. Once. And I've described it.

C.B.   Where? I can't place it.

E.I.   In *The Killer*. But nobody could understand what the radiant city mentioned in the play was. It's light, the city of light.

C.B.   I can understand why I missed the reference. It hadn't occurred to me that the radiant city was the transposition of a personal experience, because in the play it's attributed to one of your characters.

E.I.   Light is the world transfigured. It is, for instance, the glorious transformation, in the springtime, of that muddy path from my childhood. Suddenly, the world takes on an inexplicable beauty. When I was younger, I had reserves of light. But they're beginning to shrink . . . I'm moving towards the mud. I remember one day a rather pessimistic character came to visit me. At that time I was living in a ground floor flat on the Rue Claude Terrasse. My daughter was still only a baby and we didn't have much room, we'd hung her nappies up to dry inside the house. Well, this friend arrived, complaining that life was a mess, full of ugliness and sorrow, that everything was sordid, that our house was sad and ugly, and so on. . . . And I replied: 'No, I think it's very,

very beautiful; these swaddling clothes hanging from cords in the middle of the room are very beautiful.' My friend looked at me with a mixture of surprise and contempt.

'Yes,' I repeated, 'You just have to know how to look at things, how to see them. It's wonderful. Everything is miraculous, everything is a glorious epiphany, the tiniest object looks resplendent.' For it had suddenly seemed to me that those nappies on the washing line had an unexpected beauty . . . a brilliant, virgin world. I had succeeded in seeing them through a painter's eyes, seeing them in terms of light. From that moment, everything seemed beautiful, everything was transformed. Take the house opposite, for instance, it looks very ugly with its triangular windows. Yet it's filled with light, if I look at it lovingly or kindly; I mean it suddenly lights up, it's an event that takes place. It's the kind of impression anyone can have.

C.B.   Is what happens in *The Killer* the same as your experience in the Rue Claude Terrasse?

E.I.   Partly, yes. A lot of people have misunderstood *The Killer*. In the first act, Bérenger enters a radiant city. In a world that has been disfigured, he discovers a world transformed; he regains paradise after leaving the rainy town, after leaving the world of limbo.

C.B.   The worrying thing is that this paradise should be inhabited by a criminal. What, in that case, is the meaning of this precarious and luminous world?

E.I.   It's degradation, the fall.

C.B.   It's the summit.

E.I.   It's the fall.

C.B.   It's the summit, the point from which one starts to fall.

E.I.   That's right.

C.B.   Doesn't ecstasy presuppose the moment in which one falls back into the ordinary?

E.I.   Yes, it's the fall, it's original sin, in other words, a slackening of attention, of the strength with which one looks at things; or again in other words, it's losing the faculty of wonderment; oblivion; the paralysis bred by habit. Familiarity is a grey cover beneath which we hide the world's virginity; that's what original sin is about—when you know what things are, but can no longer recognize anything, can no longer recognize yourself. It's also the introduction of an evil into the world. Nobody came close to understanding the play in this way. The critics said that it was not in fact about a radiant city, or rather, that this radiant city was the modern city, industrial and technological, probably because of Le Corbusier's Radiant City in Marseilles. For me, the 'radiant' city means a city 'shining with light'. Some people also said that this radiant city was not a happy city since a criminal could enter it and flourish in it. That's quite wrong. It was a very happy city that had been entered by a destructive spirit. (The word 'destructive' is more appropriate than 'good' or 'evil'—they're very vague notions.)

C.B.   But what was the personal experience you transposed in *The Killer*?

E.I.   I was about seventeen or eighteen. I was in a provincial town. It was in June, around mid-day. I was walking down one of the streets in this very quiet town. Suddenly it seemed to me that the world was both retreating and moving closer at the same time, or rather that the world had moved away from me, that I was in another world, more mine than the old one, and infinitely more light; the dogs in the courtyards were barking as I passed by in the street, but it was as though their barking had suddenly become melodious, or fainter, as if it were muffled; it seemed to me that the sky had become extremely dense, that the light was almost palpable, that the houses had a brightness I had never seen before, an unaccustomed brightness, free from the weight of custom. It's very difficult to define it; perhaps the easiest thing to say is that I felt an enormous joy, I felt that I had understood something fundamental; that something very important had happened to me. At that moment, I said to myself 'I'm not afraid of death any more'. It felt like an absolute, a definitive truth. I told myself that later on, when I was sad or worried, I would need only to remember this moment to discover joy and serenity again. It sustained me for quite some time. Now, I've forgotten that moment. Oh, of course, I can still remember it a little, but it's just . . . well, just a theoretical memory . . . I remember those moments because I've repeated them to myself, wanted to keep them alive in my memory. But I've never managed to 'live' them again. Yes, it was a kind of miraculous moment that lasted for three or four minutes. It seemed to me there was no longer such a thing as weight. I could walk with great steps, with huge leaps, without getting tired. And then, suddenly, the world became itself again, and it still is, or almost. The washing that was drying in the yards of the little provincial houses no longer looked like banners, like pennants, but simply like old washing. The world had fallen back into a hole.

C.B.   Some of the words you used just now struck me as very significant, and suggest to me that this memory is perhaps not quite as theoretical as you say it is. You mentioned the absence of weight as being one of the characteristics of this experience, and also mentioned your disappointment, at the end, with a world that had gone back to being what it was. Aren't these precisely the two central themes of *A Stroll in the Air*, Bérenger's desire to fly off and his final disappointment, his bitterness after his flight?

E.I. Bérenger's disappointment is, perhaps, also the presence of tyranny, of blindness in the world; the world offers no resistance to a spreading stupidity. But what I wrote in *A Stroll in the Air* was rooted in dreams, in the dream of flying which is a common dream that psychiatrists interpret erotically and which I think could be interpreted as a dream of freedom and glory.

C.B. What form do these dreams of flying take?

E.I. Well, one example is climbing, which leads to flying. Though, strictly speaking, climbing isn't a dream. When I was suffering from insomnia, a friend advised me, in order to get to sleep, to imagine that I was climbing a mountain. It's really just a question of an integration technique. I tried it. I would imagine climbing up a mountain that I could see in my mind. It was very difficult at first, very painful, it was almost impossible; but then suddenly, at a given moment, near the top of the slope, it becomes quick and extremely easy. I'm climbing, taking large strides, in my imagination. Larger and larger strides: a tiny effort is enough. And I fall asleep, completely relaxed. Actually, the climb that this friend, Eliade, advised me to imagine is an archetypal dream.

C.B. That's the Eliade who's the authority on symbols and myths.

E.I. I've had other archetypal dreams, but more negative ones. Like the wall dream: when you find yourself in front of a wall and you can't get over it.
    There's also this dream I had recently. I dreamed I was a cosmonaut. I'm a funny kind of cosmonaut. I'm

inside a sort of celluloid cabin. I'm sitting naked (it's almost the foetal position, isn't it) opposite another person who looks just like me. I'm a foetus and a cosmonaut at the same time. I know that I'm travelling to another planet. There is limitless space all round our cabin. We arrive, the other man and I. We've grown and we have goggles, like the aviators wore in 1914. There's a huge crowd on the planet, an enormous number of people. Some of them have beards. In particular, there is one man with a black eye-patch on. I feel very uneasy. I say to my companion, who has now become a sort of guide, very different from myself, much more mature psychologically, 'This whole thing was a mistake. How will we manage to get back to earth?' It's very awkward. Here I am discussing this with someone on a street in another planet, though it's really just one of the outer boulevards in Paris, the Boulevard Lefèvre. This someone says to me, 'Instead of getting all worked up and morbidly upset about this, why don't you just go and get our tickets back to earth, everything will be all right, you'll see.' I go to the station, I ask the woman in the ticket office for tickets back to earth. I can't understand what this woman is saying, because she answers me in Italian. At least I know now that Martians speak Italian; that's something, at any rate. . . . So, I leave the station and try to find my travelling companion. I can't find him anywhere. I'm distraught. Alone, and lost. That's how the dream ends. To leave the earth and be unable to get back again. That's another basic anxiety.

C.B. So, what we're talking about now is the other side of the theme of light, of flying away. Despite the cosmonaut's flight, what we have here is the theme of confinement in the cabin, the theme of separation. It seems to me that, for you, joy and anguish are linked, the one with light, with the absence of weight, the other with darkness, mud, sinking in slime. Quite recently, when

I was reading *Hunger and Thirst*, I was struck by a short sentence that occurred almost parenthetically in the middle of a long speech and that reminded me of those people drowning in the pond in *The Killer* and also of that story called *Mud* in *The Colonel's Photograph*, where the fear of getting sucked into the mud is expressed in a very compelling and concrete way. It seemed to me then that *Mud* was an essential key to understanding a theme which, although it appears in your work in a variety of forms, remains essentially a single theme. In *Victims of Duty*, for example, the descent into the past is symbolized at one point by a sinking into the mud. Choubert imagines he is trapped in the mud, and the mud is rising up to his neck, his chin, his lips, whereas when he is trying to recognize himself, to recapture his identity, he mimes the movement of climbing, which ties in with that dream of integration you were talking about just now. Even in *The Bald Prima Donna*, on a very different, much more abstract level, one can see the characters foundering in their own language, in the banality of language, and this suggests their inability to keep a grip on the world. And in *Jacques*, when Roberta says that she's being bogged in, we aren't sure whether she's being sucked in by her nightmare or by her verbal delirium. All this seems to me to express the difficulty of being.

E.I. Yes, being can be difficult. . . .

C.B. So there is a definite opposition between, on the one hand, light, air, flying off, and on the other hand, thickness and heaviness, which are often linked to the theme of mud, of muddy water, even—with the pond in *The Killer*—of clear water.

E.I. I'm not sure why that water was clear. I wonder. It ought not to be. Unless . . . yes, it's clear in the beginning. It's less clear afterwards because of the drowned woman with her red hair that becomes a kind of plant and gives the pond a darker colour.

You say that in my plays there's a lot of mud, and people sinking in mud. As you say, this corresponds precisely to one of my two states of being. I feel either very heavy or very light, or else too heavy or too light. Weightlessness is that euphoric evanescence that can become tragic or sorrowful when there is any anguish. When there is no anguish, it's easy simply to be.

I don't know what a psychiatrist would say about all this. I think we've already mentioned Jung. A Jungian would say that what I write is neurotic because my writing expresses the separation of heaven and earth. Sometimes, in fact, there's heaviness, thickness—earth, water, mud—sometimes there's the sky, weightlessness, evanescence. So what I write is really the expression of an imbalance between earth and heaven, a lack of synthesis, of integration, it's the expression of a kind of neurosis.

C.B. But isn't literature sometimes a way of expressing a neurosis?

E.I. I think that literature is neurosis. If there's no neurosis, there's no literature. Health is neither poetic nor literary. And it leaves no room for progress either: it asks for 'nothing more, nothing better'. The real questions is whether this 'neurosis' is significant or representative of a human tragedy, or whether it's just an individual case. If it's an individual case, then it's certainly less interesting. To the extent that this neurosis is representative of the human condition (isn't man 'the sick animal'?), or of a metaphysical anguish, or else is the echo of psychosociological conditions which are the fault not of the writer but of objective realities, then it can be interesting, vastly significant, and it becomes crucial to explore it in depth.

So the theme of the wretchedness of man's condition

36

is perhaps experienced—well, for me in any case, and for quite a few other people as well—as weight and thickness. Of course that's individual psychology. . . . But, individual psychology is situated not only in a human context, in an extra-social and an extra-historical situation, but in a historic and social context as well; perhaps, socially speaking, this difficulty of being and this heaviness are the result of what people call totalitarianism, collectivism, the crowd, the mass, or else 'the stresses and strains of modern life', and so on. . . . Or else the totalitarianisms are themselves the thickness, the asphyxia, the oppression that the modern world inflicts upon us and that we in turn inflict upon it: tyranny and suffocation are human secretions. I think there are moments of lightness in the world: Pericles, the Renaissance; and moments of heaviness: forms of Stalinism and neo-Stalinism, right-wing Fascism and left-wing Fascism, collectivization, as well as super-capitalization, statism, nationalism. . . .

Claude Bonnefoy. Most of the literary works that you liked when you were young were impregnated with light. In this connection, you yourself have mentioned both your experiences of light and your dreams, thus underlining the fact that you approach the natural world and the cultural world in the same way, that for you there is no separation between these two worlds. But with the dreams—as it did at the time of your exile from La Chapelle-Anthenaise—the opposition between light and

darkness emerged, and also the opposition between lightness and heaviness, between happiness and anguish. These
antitheses can be found in your plays and we shall no
doubt have more than one occasion to come back to
them. But for the moment—since we're trying to discover the sources of your inspiration, or at least the
climate which made its growth possible—I should like
to know which are the writers in whom you have
recognized an experience of anguish similar to your
own, or which writers have caused a sense of anguish in
you. Aren't there some writers who seem to you to
reflect the existence of an oppressive world in which
man moves in search of light, particularly since what
interests you in this world is the fact that the people in
it are always searching for light?

Eugène Ionesco. Really, you know, I can't say that I've been
influenced by writers, or at least it seems to me that I
haven't been. But I think anyway that I have found in
certain writers the expression of my own dominant
obsessions; and in their way of expressing these obsessions I've been able to discover an affinity with myself,
a support for my own ideas, my own impressions. Or
rather, I've discovered the expression of what I thought
and felt. When something's already been well expressed,
it can be very useful. You say to yourself, 'This writer
says what I should have liked to say, what I have not
succeeded in saying'. And to this extent, other writers
can be very useful to you. Some things that I have
thought obscurely may have been expressed by other
writers in a very clear way, and the illumination these
writers provide can be a great help to me.

C.B.   Which writers have illuminated certain of your obsessions for you in this way?

E.I.   There was Kafka; *Metamorphosis* first of all, then the
whole of Kafka. There were some painters, like

Chirico. There was Borges. We feel the same kind of anguish.

C.B. Which of Borges' books in particular?

E.I. *La Biblioteca de Babel.*

C.B. Which is principally an expression of the anguish caused by civilization.

E.I. Yes, and there's something else as well: there's infinity, there's the labyrinth, which is an image of infinity, the same labyrinth that you also find in Chirico and in Kafka. The labyrinth is hell; it's time; it's space; it's infinity. Whereas paradise on the other hand is a spherical world, a total world with 'everything in it', neither finitude nor infinity, a place in which the finite-infinite problem simply does not arise. That was what La Chapelle-Anthenaise seemed to me: a place free from anguish. As soon as there's a question of dimension or duration, then you're in hell.

C.B. And what would you say you got from Kafka?

E.I. I discovered Kafka rather late. The first book of his that I read, *Metamorphosis*, made a very deep impression on me, and yet I'm not sure that, when I first read it, I really understood it. I felt that it contained something terrible, something that could happen to any of us, even though it was presented in a completely unrealistic form. The thing that struck me most, that I felt most deeply, was the guilt, a guilt without cause, a latent guilt perhaps. And still more—and this was perhaps not what Kafka wanted his story to show me—the fact that anyone can become a monster, that it's possible for all of us to become monsters. The monster in us can rise up. We can take on the monster's face. In other words, the monster in us can get the upper hand, the way crowds or whole nations can become dehumanized from time to time. Wars, uprisings, pogroms, collective frenzies and collective crimes, tyrannies and oppressions: these are just some aspects of the revelation of our monstrousness, aspects that occur to me because they're common, right now, or in history. Our monstrousness has countless faces, collective or otherwise, striking or less striking, obvious or less obvious.

C.B.   You say that this is not perhaps exactly what Kafka meant to say in his story. . . . In any case, it's easy to see what you saw Kafka to mean, what it was you found in him. When you talk about *Metamorphosis*, you're also giving us an outline of *Rhinoceros*.

E.I.   Of course. The awakening of the monster—that's in Kafka too. When I read Kafka, I was living in a kind of panic. And again now, it seems to me that at certain moments anyone at all can become a criminal. You never know what might happen, whether the monster in you isn't going to awaken and rise up. This idea has caused me considerable anguish.

C.B.   Besides Kafka and Borges, are there any other writers who have made a similar impression on you?

E.I.   Other writers have made an impression on me, but a quite different kind of impression. Dostoyevsky, of course. Proust, enormously. Proust because he wrote about things I'd felt and had not yet managed to put into words. For instance, I've walked past a house whose kitchen window was open and there's been a smell of baking that has reminded me of something else which in its turn reminded me of something else, and so on. I didn't know how to formulate this, I thought it was impossible to put it into words until I read the famous passage in Proust about the madeleine.

C.B.   What about Valéry?

E.I.   No. His works don't have that inner light, just a metallic light that's hard and cold, a diamond-like light. Valéry Larbaud seems to me much more affective—either that, or his affectiveness is much more obvious. Since I'm more affective than cerebral I was moved by him, by Alain-Fournier, by Gérard de Nerval, by the lyrical side of Proust. . . . To be honest, some writers have sustained me, driven me, helped me, enlightened me, have made me feel justified in what I was doing, and they've done this on two levels: the emotional and the cerebral level. Actually, affectiveness is a kind of thought, just as cerebration is also emotional. One should leave the task of separating them to the logicians and the psychologists. In a general way, although affectivity and logic overlap—even mathematics is subjective, since it's a set of structures in my mind—there are two kinds of writers who have influenced me: poets, and a few thinkers.

C.B.   Who in the 'thinkers' category?

E.I.   Dionysius the Areopagite. Is he a mystic, a philosopher, or a poet? What are his ideas? They're the expression of his experience, of an experience that goes beyond ordinary ideas. I've never attained this very high form of experience myself, but in a sense the Areopagite gave me some notion of what it was like living beyond ordinary ideas, beyond the impulses of a normal human heart and mind. So I can speak of him as someone who had an influence on me. In the same way, I can speak not of Saint John of the Cross but of Jean Baruzi's book about Saint John of the Cross. It showed me the kind of experience Saint John had had, something very close to the experience of the Byzantine mystics. In his case, they are the revelations of the night, that is, if I remember correctly, the denial of the world of the senses and the rejection of the image in order to attain a light beyond the image, a light without image. In fact, even though I don't remember the Byzantine texts, of Gregory and a lot of others, very exactly, despite their rejection of the physical world and the image, what stays with me from them is an image—an image without an image, an image of light. You find the same thing again in a book called *The Philokalia*, some extracts from which have been translated into French and English. From this experience, from the experience of all these people who rejected the physical world with all its brightness, its colour and light, what remains paradoxically is light, brightness, vividness. Wouldn't you agree?

C.B. Depending on whether you're a neo-Platonist or a Christian, it's the light of the One or the light of God.

E.I. That's it, whether you're a neo-Platonist, a neo-Christian, a neo-Jew, or even a Marxist, since we all know that if it hadn't been for the Jewish tradition, Marx would never have become what he is today. Actually, in Marxism, apart from some conclusions that were justified in the context of a certain social situation that existed in the nineteenth century but which has now been superceded, you also find nostalgia for the lost paradise. It has transmitted this nostalgia at second hand to the revolutionaries who don't know exactly what it's all about but who are none the less seeking the lost light. It's the only justification for Communism. From time to time something extraordinary happens that reveals what lies behind Marxism. That's when you discover the myth, the deep, essential truth, beneath the ideology; for ideology is simply a degradation of mythical truth.

C.B. Then you attach a lot of importance to myths as well as dreams?

E.I.   Yes. I'm thinking now about a Russian film, *Pinocchio*. *Pinocchio* was originally an Italian children's story. It's been the basis for a lot of films. Walt Disney made a silly film out of it. A Russian made a film of it that was equally silly in one sense, but in another sense, not silly at all. I mean that the director was intelligent in spite of himself, in spite of his ideology. Quite simply, *Pinocchio* is the story of an old man who makes wooden dolls. And one of these wooden dolls comes to life. Why does it come to life? Because this poor old man, this pathetic Pygmalion, loves this doll, his child, so much that his love gives it life. That's the starting point of the Italian story.

C.B.   Has this any connection with the Jewish myth of the Golem?

E.I   No, no obvious connection, at any rate. Pygmalion, the Golem and Pinocchio might inspire an academic to write a doctoral thesis on the theme of the statue that comes to life. But I'd rather tell you what happens in the Russian film. In it, this poor little child, or rather this poor little doll, is exploited by a wicked capitalist who owns a circus. The doll is somehow alienated because he is exploited. He grows human as soon as he achieves freedom and manages to run away from the circus. Where does he run to? Towards the Soviet paradise. So Pinocchio escapes. He takes a boat. The wicked capitalist follows him in another boat. Then, suddenly, Pinocchio takes off and flies away and there's an extraordinary scene of his flight through the sky. All the mystic themes, and in particular the mystic feelings for light and freedom come together in the images—with their almost virgin, wonderfully fresh colours—of this film which was only made because it was supposed to illustrate an ideology. But behind this ideology, you can recognize the theme of ascension, the themes of sky, light and paradise. And 'real' life as well: Pinocchio's

43

wooden body is transformed into a human body, a 'corps de gloire'.[1] Pinocchio arrives in a flowery heaven which is presided over by a smiling old man with a moustache, who's supposed to be that pig Stalin, but who, for the purposes of the story, is transformed into none other than God the Father. Now don't you agree that Marxism contains within it the myth of the New Jerusalem, of the ideal City?

C.B. And it's not surprising that the great Marxist philosopher Ernst Bloch should have been interested in Münzer, one of the principal creators of the revolutionary Millenarian movement of the Renaissance. But to get back to the point. Starting with literature and moving on to the Byzantine mystics, you've shown us with the Russian film about Pinocchio the resurgence, or rather the permanence, of the theme of paradise lost and of the quest for the light. But what seems to me more important here, something that helps us to understand the way you write and feel, and consequently to come to an understanding of your work, is that you avoid any classifications that rigidify ideas; and that, when you speak about what has influenced you, you don't confine yourself simply to literature but put on the same level—or at least mention in the same breath—both literary and mystical works, both poets and philosophers, your own experiences and traditional myths. In all this there is a very characteristic effort to get back to essentials, to the great themes that are at the roots of the most varied forms of artistic, philosophical and literary expression. It seems to me that in literature, mysticism and philosophy you look for the same thing you do in your dreams, namely the great archetypal myths. It is therefore not surprising that your plays should often be, albeit in a camouflaged form, illustrations of a myth.

But we'll come back to this later. For the moment, we

[1] NOTE: a phrase used in the French catechism to describe the body of Christ.

44

should get back to the subject of literature and to the poets and thinkers who have influenced you.

E.I. There are poets and thinkers. And there are also critics. Among these, I think I should mention Paulhan and his book *Les Fleurs de Tarbes*.

C.B. What was it you learnt from *Les Fleurs de Tarbes*?

E.I. I learned a lot. Among other things, that there's nothing to be learned from critics; that what critics write about the present is almost always repudiated, in one way or another, by future critics; that you ultimately have to admit that criticism is a question of intuition, that this intuition is very rare and impossible to define; that having a feeling for literary quality is like having an ear for music; that the real critic is either someone who through any one work of literature discovers the essence of literature, or poetry, or poetic quality; or else someone who rediscovers the essence of literature intuitively, in a work that expresses it. I learned that a literary vocation, besides being something very rare, is also innate, congenital: you can tell at a very early age which children will be scientists or writers or politicians; at the age of five, Mozart was assimilating music and also discovering it in himself, re-inventing it.

But this isn't exactly what *Les Fleurs de Tarbes* is about.

C.B. We seem to be getting back to the problem of literary criticism, to the problem of the meaning of literature which we were discussing in connection with your years at university.

E.I. There's a kind of literary criticism that claims to be scientific because it's on the periphery of literature, because it isn't literature, and confines itself to a study of the author's biography, to exploring the historical and social context, to substituting psychoanalysis for an attempt at understanding a work, understanding what makes it unique. Yet every work is a unique thing, a complete world, a cosmos. A work is important only in so far as it's unique. And since it is unique, it is hard to understand. When you confront a new work, through its world, you must every time be able to discover *the* world. . . . That's why good critics are very rare. I think I've said this before: you need talent to be a writer, but to be a critic you need genius.

C.B. Do you think that apart from *Les Fleurs de Tarbes*, there were any literary essays or critical works that taught you something about the mechanics of creation, about literary structures, or basically, about what literature is?

E.I. Croce possibly, and . . . Fénéon . . . whom Paulhan saved from oblivion. It's easier to learn what literature isn't. The great critics are all artists . . . like Delacroix; like Apollinaire, and Baudelaire, and Boileau, and the discoverer-side of Cocteau, and Gide, and Proust . . . or else non-philosophical critics, like Thibaudet. Sometimes they're even philosophers: Freud, who revolutionized people's understanding of Sophocles, and of so many other writers; and then Heidegger. . . . But you need to be a great philosopher and not just a philosophy student, like all those hard-working scholars who are encumbered rather than helped by all their sociologico-psychologico-Marxist baggage. . . . But there have always been pedants, learned asses.

C.B. Don't all these things—literary criticism, literary analysis, the question of knowing what literature is or should be—boil down to the eternal debate about the usefulness of literature?

E.I. That's a question I asked myself a long time ago, when I first started writing. I was twenty at the time, maybe twenty-two. I said: 'Literature serves no purpose. It's

46

not worth taking it seriously'. I indulged in all kinds of elaborate jokes. For instance I used to produce lengthy studies of the most important Rumanian authors which proved that they were all worthless. And people would write answers to these very violent pamphlets, they'd take them perfectly seriously. There were vast numbers of critics and counter-critics, all anxious to prove that I was wrong. And when the controversy had died down, I'd write another series of articles saying that the poets I had denigrated were really great poets. Naturally people found this somewhat surprising. I replied that on the one hand there are no criteria in criticism, that one can say anything, argue, explain, justify any position; and that on the other hand, even if there were criteria, it was of little importance since literature was not a thing to be taken seriously. Madame Hélène Vianou published a study of my first Rumanian articles in the *Revue des Sciences Humaines*. My articles were extremely badly written, but I was trying to say precisely what everyone is beginning to say nowadays about how un-serious literature is. Well, not really. . . . Sometimes I think literature isn't a serious thing, that it's not worth giving your life for it or dying for it; sometimes I think it is serious.

C.B. How would you answer Rilke's question: 'Would you die if you weren't allowed to write?'

E.I. No, No, of course not. But I'd be very unhappy, because literature is my whole life really.

C.B. We've been discussing literature. You've mentioned a certain number of writers, poets, philosophers and critics who have influenced or at any rate impressed you. What surprises me is that you haven't mentioned a single dramatist.

E.I. I could say that I don't like my fellow playwrights, that

I'm an intuitive playwright. But I'm just joking. What was your question again? Why haven't I mentioned any dramatists? Perhaps because I never needed plays, never needed to discover the theatre through other writers, because I think the theatre is in me!

C.B. But were you indifferent to the great dramatists?

E.I. Naturally I was taught French literature and I read Corneille, Racine and Molière. Well, not really. Corneille, Racine and Molière were explained to me, I was made to read a few of the plays and also, as one does in school, to read a few scenes from some of their other plays. But I don't think I've ever sat down and really read Racine from beginning to end the way some people have. And if you do read Racine or Corneille—well, what a disaster Corneille is! I could never read plays, I found it very boring. I used to read novels, poetry, books with ideas in them.

C.B. But really not a single dramatist?

E.I. Shakespeare. Not Molière. My daughter loves Molière. When she was nine or ten she was already reading Molière and enjoying it enormously. Personally, I never took to Molière. Now I'm beginning to enjoy him more.

C.B. Why is that?

E.I. Because people often thought that the *précieux* and *précieuses* were more intelligent than Molière and that in spite of his talent Molière was just a poor bastard, that he had a bourgeois mentality. But I think really that Molière and sometimes Aristophanes were right, and that the philosophers and the 16th *arrondissement*[1] were wrong. There was certainly a 16th *arrondissement*

[1] NOTE: the expensive 'snob' neighbourhood in Paris.

48

in the days of Louis XIV and possibly even in Athenian society.

C.B.   Agathon's dinner-parties, you mean?

E.I.   Well, the pedants and *précieux* in every age have all maintained that comic writers were idiots, albeit inspired idiots. For them, Aristophanes and Molière were idiots. But you know how fatuous the *précieux*, the knowing asses and all the other Bartholomeuses are: because they're complicated, they think they must be complex; because they're unclear, they think they must be difficult. I think we need to revise the stale old notion that comic writers are all simpletons. After all, a wise ass is better than an ignorant one.

C.B.   I'd like to get back to Shakespeare. What is it he represents for you? What are your reasons for considering him an outstanding dramatist?

E.I.   Outstanding, yes. But more important, a dramatist we can understand today. Didn't he say of the world that 'it is a tale told by an idiot' and that everything is but 'sound and fury'? He's the forefather of the theatre of the absurd. He said it all, and said it a long time ago. Beckett tries to repeat him. I don't even try: since he said so well what he had to say, what can we possibly add?

C.B.   You have often been compared to Feydeau. Did he or did he not have an influence on your writing?

E.I.   I've already told you, I'm far more influenced by poets and novelists than I am by dramatists. This sounds as though it isn't true. But in fact it's absolutely true. People had told me I was influenced by Strindberg. So then I read Strindberg's plays and said, 'They're right, I *am* influenced by Strindberg'. People had told me I was influenced by Vitrac. So I read Vitrac and said, 'They're right, I *am* influenced by Vitrac'. People had told me I was influenced by Feydeau and Labiche. So I read Feydeau and Labiche and said, 'They're right, I *am* influenced by Feydeau and Labiche'. That's how I came to read so many plays. But, if I was 'influenced' by these writers without ever having read them, it simply proves that an individual is not alone. There's a completely false belief that people decide, consciously and deliberately, to do or not do certain things. Whereas in fact all the preoccupations, obsessions and universal problems are inside us and we all of us discover them in turn. The great mistake of comparative literature—at least the way it was twenty years ago—was its belief that influences are consciously assimilated, even its belief that influences exist. When quite often influences do not exist. Things are simply there. Several of us react to them in the same way. We are both free and determined at the same time.

C.B.   Now that you have read Feydeau, what's your opinion of him?

E.I.   He's a *great* comic writer. But for me personally, not very interesting. I personally am bored by him, just as I'm bored by Labiche. But he was a great writer all the same. He was a natural humorist. He wasn't concerned with literature or philosophical mish-mash. He had no cultural aspirations. He was what he was: a natural dramatist, a theatrical giant.

C.B.   But haven't certain common tricks of staging provided objective proof of the similarity between Feydeau and yourself? Doesn't the way in which certain of Feydeau's plays are staged nowadays, with the emphasis on the mechanical quality of the language and the plot, owe a good deal to the production style of, for instance, *The Bald Prima Donna*?

E.I. I don't think so. If the actors who performed my other plays had a recognizable style, the ones who performed *The Bald Prima Donna* did not. What they did—and it was very effective—was to perform a work with ridiculous dialogue quite naturally and seriously, the way they would if they were in a conventional *boulevard* production. But to get back to this question of the mechanical qualities of Feydeau's plays: quite recently, I read one of his plays, *A Flea in Her Ear*, extremely carefully. I can hardly remember the plot at all. What was interesting was the mechanics of the plot. People have talked a lot about Feydeau's clockwork style, but I don't think anyone has really analysed it sufficiently. People have also claimed that his plays contain a critique, or at least a scathing portrait, of the society of his time. In fact, as far as content is concerned, his plays are entirely devoid of interest, they're stupid. But their mechanics *are* interesting: the mechanics of proliferation, of geometric progression, mechanics or patterns for their own sake. We all know at least one famous remark of Bergson's, that 'the comic is something mechanical encrusted on the living'. Feydeau (in *A Flea in Her Ear*) starts out with something living and a very small element of the mechanical; then the mechanical element takes over until there's nothing left but the machine alone, wild, quite out of control. A machine that gets out of control is a machine that works too well, so well that everything is turned into part of the machine; it takes over everything, the whole world gets sucked into its mechanism. I maintain that you find the same thing in my plays, in *The Chairs*, it's a mechanical chaos;[1] in *The New Tenant* it's the same thing; whereas in *The Lesson* it's language that gets out of control. You see, the comic is terrifying, the comic is tragic.

C.B. If I understand you correctly, other dramatists have very

[1] NOTE: Ionesco's phrase 'dérèglement mécanique' is virtually untranslatable.

little influence on you, but basically what has affected your progress as a writer has been your own ideas about literary aesthetics in general and, more particularly—to mention two of the dominant characteristics of your plays—about the meaning of the comic and the significance of dreams. And any affinity that one can observe between your plays and those of established writers is essentially due to the fact that you have rediscovered certain fundamental procedures of dramatic writing rather than to any direct or conscious influences.

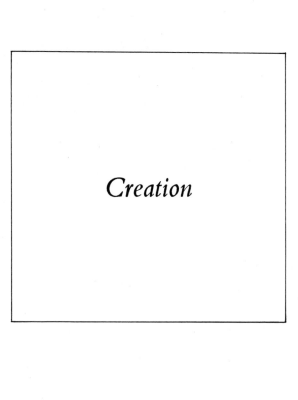

Creation

Claude Bonnefoy. Bearing in mind what you've told us about your tastes, I can't help wondering how and why you happened to become a playwright.

Eugène Ionesco. It puzzles me as well. You'd do better to ask a psychologist about it. Why *did* I write my first play? Perhaps it was to prove that nothing had any real importance, that everything was unlivable—literature, drama, life, human values, they were all unlivable.

C.B. But you could have chosen to express this in another literary form—a poem, a novel or an essay. Certain of your plays like *The Killer, Victims of Duty, Rhinoceros* and *A Stroll in the Air* were originally short stories that you've now published in a single volume called *The Colonel's Photograph*. Wasn't your vocation originally more that of a storyteller?

E.I. As I've already told you, I started by writing literary criticism. And poems, very bad poems.

C.B. Should I contradict you?

E.I. Oh, they're really pitiful, full of a primitive anthropomorphism: flowers weeping and bleeding and dreaming of meadows and springtime and heaven knows what else. I was only seventeen. It wasn't all my fault, Maeterlinck and Francis Jammes were partly to blame. Anyway, after I'd written some very bad poems, I started writing extremely harsh criticism, as though I was trying to punish myself by punishing other people. After that, I tried to write a novel. It was all a long, long time ago.

C.B.   What was the novel about?

E.I.   About me, of course.

C.B.   So you started out in the classic adolescent way by writing poems?

E.I.   No, I'd already written some plays before that.

C.B.   Already?

E.I.   Well, let me see . . . first of all, when I was about ten or eleven, I started to write my *Memoirs*. I wrote two pages, but I've now lost them both. I can still remember the first page, the first sentences. I described how I'd had my photograph taken at the age of three. Now, of course, I've forgotten what it was like having my photo taken at the age of three. I can only remember being ten and writing down what it was like. And when I was eleven, I wrote poetry and some patriotic plays. *French* patriotic plays. When I was thirteen, I moved to Rumania and learned Rumanian, and when I was fourteen, I translated my patriotic play and turned it into a Rumanian patriotic play.

C.B.   One could say you were doubly patriotic.

E.I.   Actually, I was very confused as a child. At primary school, in France, I'd been taught that French—which was my language—was the most beautiful language in the world, that the French were the bravest people in the world, that they'd always defeated their enemies, that if they had on occasion been defeated themselves, it was because the odds had been ten-to-one against them or because of a few individuals like Grouchy at Waterloo and Bazaine in the Franco-Prussian war. When I got to Bucharest, my teachers explained that my language was Rumanian, that the most beautiful language in the world was not French but Rumanian, that the Rumanians had always defeated their enemies, that if they hadn't always been victorious it was because they'd had people like Grouchy and Bazaine—I can't even remember their names—on their side. So I learned that it was not the French but the Rumanians who were the best people, superior to everyone else. It's a good thing I didn't move to Japan the year after that. . . . So, I began by writing a patriotic play. And I also wrote a comic play at the same time.

C.B.   You were always drawn towards comedy, then?

E.I.   Yes. But my memory of the play is very hazy. I was eleven or twelve years old at the time and it was set in Paris, on the Rue de l'Avre. A child, one of my school-friends, had told me that he could make a film because he had a camera, which in fact wasn't true. He was a little mythomaniac. He'd asked me to write a script for him. What I do remember is that it ended with the characters smashing everything in the house. Seven or eight children were sitting having their tea together, and afterwards they smashed their cups, they smashed all the crockery, they smashed up all the furniture and threw their parents out of the windows.

C.B.   I suppose it couldn't have ended with an atom bomb, like *Anger*. But it's curious to discover in this childhood script the same patterns and themes that one finds in *Anger*: acceleration, proliferation and destruction.

E.I.   Perhaps I've always thought along the same lines. You get the same thing in Feydeau too, the same acceleration and proliferation; maybe it goes back to his childhood as well. Acceleration and proliferation are probably a part of my personal rhythm, of the way I see things.

C.B. Were they also present in the novel that you'd started?

E.I. No. Definitely not.

C.B. Was it a fear of exposing yourself, a fear of being recognized that made you stop work on this novel, whose subject, you say, was yourself?

E.I. Possibly.

C.B. In the theatre, on the other hand, because of the characters, you can wear a mask even when you're talking about yourself.

E.I. What irritates me is that, increasingly, when I write anything new, everyone—academics, psychologists and so on—ferrets about to find evidence that it's me who's talking. Every day it's brought home to me more and more clearly that my plays can be seen as a series of confessions in which I give voice to my most unspeakable thoughts. People send me doctoral theses, they send me unpublished books about myself and I am absolutely terrified. Did I really have all these hidden meanings? Did I really hope that people wouldn't understand or that they'd put all the blame on my characters? I also realize that I've said certain things without intending to. And it's other people who discover all the things that I wasn't really aware of: it's insane. For the sake of clarity, I ought to say that my characters are not always 'alter-egos'; they're other people, as well, imaginary people; they're also caricatures of myself, of what I've been frightened of becoming, of what I could have—but fortunately didn't—become; or else they're simply en-

58

largements of different facets of myself; or else—and I'm repeating myself deliberately—they're other people, people I pity, people I laugh at, people I hate or love; sometimes, but more rarely, they are people I should have liked to be. They are also the personifications of a kind of anguish. And quite often, too, they are characters from my dreams.

C.B. If writing was a way of liberating yourself from certain things, didn't it upset you to rediscover these things in the distorting mirrors of other people's criticism?

E.I. Yes, it did.

C.B. So there's the danger that what starts out as a liberation can cease to be one as a result of this mirror of criticism.

E.I. Yes, In fact, you could say that everything shared this danger, but only if everyone were a poet or an artist, or else a psychiatrist or a priest. But as most people have the mentality of a concierge, or else are society people, which is to say, simply concierges further up the social ladder, literature is constantly being undressed. The whole of literary history as we know it is just back-stairs snooping. Journalists and readers don't understand what a man says in the same way an artist would, or a priest, or a doctor or a psychologist. They don't see the meaning of these confessions, they don't understand the deepest or most universal truth of an individual confession. What interests them isn't the universal truth but the personal confession—looking through the keyhole, in other words. What interests people is not what's universal or general in a writer's work, but knowing about his private life. In other words, everything but the work itself. Of course, it's interesting to study sources, but it's more interesting to study the work itself. A work is more than the sum of its causes, it goes beyond them.

C.B. What I find interesting is the reverse—I want to find out how and why you came to put on the mask of playwright.

E.I. How I came to the theatre? Quite simply, I don't know.

C.B. Didn't you say in *Notes and Counter-Notes* that you became a playwright because you didn't like the theatre?

E.I. Yes. But that answer was by way of a simplification.

C.B. Yet it was consistent with the subtitle of *The Bald Prima Donna*—an 'anti-play'. What exactly did you mean by the term 'anti-play'?

E.I. I must have known what it meant fifteen or so years ago when I wrote the play. But I've forgotten since then.

C.B. Because, in the interim, you've begun to like the theatre?

E.I. Oh, I've talked of liking the theatre, but it wasn't entirely true. I haven't ever really liked it. I'll admit frankly that when I wrote in *L'Expérience du Théâtre*[1] that at a certain point I discovered the theatre and discovered I liked it, this was a concession I made for the benefit of the theatre critics who defended me and the actors who performed my plays.

C.B. When you wrote your first play, *The Bald Prima Donna*, you must have had certain specific aims. What struck the critics—I'm not talking about the ones who completely missed the point—was an essential criticism of everyday existence that involved a basic questioning of literary language.

E.I. I don't know what they saw in the play. There was one

[1] NOTE: translated by L. C. Prouko in the *Tulane Drama Review*, September 1959 under the title *Discovering the Theatre*.

man who understood it very well. That was Jean Pouillon. In June 1950 he wrote a piece in *Les Temps Modernes* which gave an excellent account of what I had tried to do. It was exactly right. I wasn't concerned with the impossibility of communication or with solitude. Quite the contrary. I am in favour of solitude. People have described my plays as laments of the solitary man unable to communicate with other people. That's quite wrong. It's easy to communicate. Man is never really alone; and if he's unhappy, it's because he's never really alone.

C.B. Is that what you were hoping to show?

E.I. What did I mean that play to be? It was an expression of the unexpected, of existence seen as something absolutely unpredictable. There *is* a degree of communication between people. They talk to one another. They understand one another. That's what is so astounding. How is it possible for people to understand one another? It's the fact that we do understand one another that I don't understand. If, intentionally, you put yourself completely outside everything, or one floor above what's going on, if you look at people as though they were part of a show and you yourself were a being from another world, looking down on what's happening here, then you wouldn't understand anything, words would be hollow, everything would be empty. You can get this feeling if you block your ears when you're watching people dancing. What are they doing? What can it possibly mean? Their movements are senseless. I write plays to express this feeling of astonishment, this feeling of amazement. Why and what are we? What does it mean? No, I don't even wonder why, I don't even ask what it means. My question is unformulated, but all the more forceful for that, a sort of absolutely basic, fundamental feeling aroused by the fact that something is there which moves, or seems to be moving. This is what I wanted to convey. Naturally people came up with sociological interpretations, but what I really wanted to express was something which lay outside the boundaries of logic and sociology. It was like beaming a spotlight on humanity, on the amazingness of people generally, all mixed up with my astonishment at existence itself. Everywhere there's a cause for amazement: in language, in picking up a glass of something, in draining it at a single gulp, in the mere fact of existing, of being. Going for a walk, not going for a walk, it's astonishing. Doing something, not doing something; astonishing. Having revolutions, not having revolutions; astonishing. Once people have accepted existence, once they've moved inside it, everything stops being amazing or absurd. Once they've accepted the idea of being on the inside, they start to communicate. When you step outside, move away and take a good look, you stop communicating. The characters in *The Bald Prima Donna* all talked in platitudes. But I really didn't write the play to criticize the banality of what they were saying. What they said didn't seem banal to me but astonishing and extraordinary to the highest degree. When, at the beginning of the play, Mr. and Mrs. Smith say: 'This evening for supper we had soup, fish, cold ham and mashed potatoes . . . a very good meal . . .', I wanted to express the amazement I felt at this extraordinary act. Eating seemed to me inconceivable, astounding, overwhelming. Whether the characters say 'this evening for supper we had soup . . .' or whether they say 'there is a noumenal reality that the phenomenon conceals or, on the contrary, the essence of things may be expressed, or known, precisely thanks to the phenomenon', it all has an equal value, or non-value, for me—both these statements are equally overwhelming. Or equally marvellous.

C.B. You place contradictory things on the same level. Doesn't the theatre, in fact, make it possible to represent these contradictions without proposing a synthesis?

E.I.   Yes, it does. And for me, and for you as well, existence is sometimes unbearable, crushing, painful, heavy and stupefying, and sometimes it seems to be the manifestation of God himself, all light. If I have written plays rather than novels, or essays, it's because essays and even novels presuppose coherent ideas, whereas 'incoherence' or contradictions can be given free rein in a play. In a play, the characters can say anything, any kind of absurdity, all the nonsense that comes into their heads, because it's not me who's saying it, it's my characters. No-one need take offence.

C.B.   So the characters in your plays enable you to keep your distance from certain problems.

E.I.   Yes, from all obsessions, all the most contradictory things. These things all come together again later on in a particular way, and constitute a synthesis . . . no, not a synthesis, a totality that somehow evens out the pros and cons, the high and the low, a totality that reconciles opposites, not in a synthesis but in multiple coexistences.

C.B.   This distance which you achieve in your plays from your obsessions, from experience, from the contradictions of existence, is noticeable when one compares the stories collected under the title *The Colonel's Photograph* with the plays you have adapted from them. In the stories, the reader feels that you are giving him the direct, or barely transposed, notation of your personal experiences, your dreams and nightmares. Whereas in the plays, one feels that you are simply showing the way it happened—with its own hidden or formal system of symbols—something that characters who are not Eugène Ionesco are living out before our eyes.

E.I.   Of course, there's a greater objectification. Only, it isn't entirely conscious. All creation is a mixture of consciousness and spontaneity.

C.B. How did the transitions from story to play take place?

E.I. The story is sometimes the starting point for the play. Though in fact, I began by writing plays. Then I wrote stories, and then more plays came out of these stories. Reading through one of my stories, I'd sometimes say to myself, this story is good, it seems to me eminently theatrical. I ought to make a play of it. When this happens, the story is the raw material, the first draft. I use it like a scenario. I can also try to make a theatrical work out of an apparently non-theatrical story, or one that is not obviously suited to theatre. The story itself is already an effort, a transcription, and the play is a transcription of this transcription. That's why there's a certain objectification.

C.B. What is the story a transcription of?

E.I. What is any poem a transcription of? What is any play that doesn't start from a basic scenario a transcription of? All literature is the transcription or record of what I see and what I think.

C.B. Could we perhaps try here, on the basis of this double transcription of story and scenario, to analyse what are for you the mechanics of creation?

E.I. Too complicated . . . for the moment. I've already written something about this, in *L'Auteur et ses Problèmes*, in the *Revue de Métaphysique*, in *Notes and Counter-Notes*.

C.B. We could try.

E.I. To try, I'd need to have a good memory.

C.B. Let us take as an example the story *The Stroller in the Air* on which one of your plays is based. What made you want to write this story? Where did the initial idea come from?

E.I. From a dream. I used one of my dreams. The one about flying. I think we've already talked about this type of dream. Anyway, at the root of this story there is on the one hand a dream, a dream of liberation and of power; and on the other, a criticism, a satire and a realistic description of the nightmare life under a totalitarian regime, a prophecy of calamity. Parisian critics—except for a few like Kanters, Lemarchand and Gautier—completely failed to understand this story, although it's really very simple. The 'highbrow' critics didn't want to understand it.

But let's get back to the play. My starting point was both a dream and a conscious thought. The dream part was the man flying. The conscious part was what he sees as a result of this flight. And what does he see? Quite simply, what's going on in half the world, and what the other half, out of blindness, indifference or obstinacy, doesn't want to see: dozens of millions of people humiliated; terror enthroned, tyranny, power gone mad, the regular little everyday apocalypse, men licking idols' arses, and other things that are catastrophically amusing. All that is already in the story. What you want to know, I suppose, is how the story became a play? I know *why*, but I no longer clearly remember how. I know why, because I simply said this to myself, *The Stroller in the Air* is not theatrical, in fact it's just the opposite, and since it's just the opposite, let's try and turn it into a play. Even the opposite of theatre can become theatre. It was a challenge. I'd already expressed my amazement and stupefaction at the fact of existence: starting from these states of mind implied making theatre out of the non-theatrical, as I'd done in *The Bald Prima Donna*. How could I make a play out of *The Stroller*, out of a man flying off and passers-by telling stories, rather than out of simple, present conflicts? That was what tempted me.

C.B. Because you thought that this impossibility was possible?

E.I. A very long time ago, I read some short stories by Jean Richepin. One of these stories was about a strange criminal who, when he was in prison, tried to compose a whole poem, an epic, with lines made up only of one-syllable words. He began to write this poem and he stopped when he realized that it really was possible. This is somewhat the same kind of challenge that I felt with several of my plays, *The Bald Prima Donna*, *A Stroll in the Air* and even *The Chairs*. Finding theatricality in its opposite, or what seems to be its opposite, is an exercise in artistic control.

C.B. Did you feel that *A Stroll in the Air* was non-theatrical because it was impossible to do?

E.I. To do in the theatre. I'm exaggerating a little. In reality everything is a drama, only it needn't be a drama in the accepted, theatrical sense. If I say my endeavour was anti-theatrical, it's because I was looking for the theatrical elsewhere than in the theatre or in theatricality—because I was looking for the dramatic situation in its original truth, a fundamental truth.

C.B. Could you define what you understand by this dramatic situation—how it differs from those classical theatrical situations that have been classified by theoreticians of dramatic art and which our teachers rammed down our throats when we were at school?

E.I. You know the answer better than I do. As I've already said, it's essentially the fact of realizing that one's human, of feeling oneself here in this situation, face to face with a world that I scarcely ever feel is *mine*, an uncomfortable but primordial and fundamental situation. The different aspects, the historical variants assumed by this world before me, behind me, above, below me, in which I flounder like someone drowning in the ocean—these different aspects, what is happening in it, that's just secondary; that is to say, whether it's this or that . . . this film or that film . . . the extraordinary thing is that there's a film, any film at all; the incredible thing is that there is such a thing as cinema; it isn't any single film that's revealing, it's the cinema. Of course it's true, right now, that newsreels are particularly exciting. But the cinema is even more exciting, the cinema is all the films there are. The cinema . . . or rather, I'm sorry, the theatre through every play . . . because we're talking about the theatre, about existence, about the fact that there is a universe, that things happen in it. Anyhow, you know what I mean.

Claude Bonnefoy. Whether your plays are based on a story or not, what is it that actually makes you write them?

Eugène Ionesco. There are moments when I think rather incoherently and loosely, when I associate images more freely, when I feel different impulses which can either co-exist or clash. When I'm in this semi-chaotic state, it's often ('often' and not 'always', because there is no absolute rule) the moment when I have to write a play: the chaos must take on a shape; a clear, coherent universe must rise out of it. But when I write articles or essays, then I feel much more in control of myself, more sure of what I think I know. I know, I'm no longer trying to know. And when that's the case, I can't write a play.

As soon as I start thinking about my plays, about other people's plays, about painting or anything else, it means I'm not in a creative period. The creative period comes when my mental metabolism goes haywire, when I function erratically or abnormally. At such moments I could write poetry if I wrote poems. Inside these moments all kinds of things loom up, the way they do at night. I don't know where they come from. I seize them as best I can. I stand them up facing each other, etc. . . . Once these things have been written down, have solidified, once they have acquired some sort of coherence through the fact that they have jelled, become linked to one another, then I can start to 'think', as they say, although, for me, thinking 'clearly' is very often thinking in a completely conventional or inadequate way, according to established clichés, according to the mechanisms of apparent rationality, and is therefore 'not thinking'.

C.B. So that your point of departure for writing a play is really a sort of incoherence, or imbalance. . . .

E.I. Of imbalance, exactly.

C.B. And this imbalance corresponds, really, to a fundamental questioning. It is itself a question, and writing for the theatre helps you if not to resolve, then at least to formulate this question.

E.I. Exactly.

C.B. So you create your balance out of imbalance.

E.I. Yes. At a certain point things seem clear to me. I can talk more easily but I don't write. At other times, it's much as though there were an earthquake in my microcosm, as though everything were collapsing, and it's a kind of night-time, or rather a mixture of light and darkness, a world of chaos. It is from this that creation arises, as it

68

did with the great macrocosm. . . . On the level of artistic creation, it's a genesis too. It's somewhat the same process, 'mutatis mutandis', but in its own image.

C.B. Does this state—with the impressions and questions it presupposes—last for as long as it takes you to write the play, that is, for several months, a year or more?

E.I. I write a play in two or three months, in a month.

C.B. And does this initial state last for these two or three months?

E.I. More or less.

C.B. Don't you have any rough spells and set-backs, good times and bad ones?

E.I. It's very hard to say. Yes, there are interruptions. I return to a more balanced, more normal state. Then I'm plunged down again. Then it's all right. But I remember what it was like when I wrote *The Chairs, How to Get Rid of It, Victims of Duty*. For instance I think I understand *Victims of Duty* very well, better than the critics did; but while I was writing these plays and even immediately afterwards, on another level of understanding, I didn't always see them very clearly.

C.B. Can you explain this mechanism, of both creation and of . . .?

E.I. Of release, at the same time. That's what it is, release. If, while I was writing it, someone had said to me, 'explain *Victims of Duty* to me', I would have had to write another play to explain it, that is to say, I would have had to write another series of images. Everyday understanding is on another level of consciousness, another level of thought, another system of formulation.

69

C.B. Choubert's adventure in *Victims of Duty* is yours too in a certain sense. You were both in the same tunnel.

E.I. Exactly. When the play is acted and the critics say 'it's this' or 'it's that', I pull myself together and shout: 'They really don't understand a thing! This is what it means', and I can explain the play. I can do it because I'm no longer in the same world, I've acquired a degree of detachment from the play. Whereas when I was writing it, I was governed by the extra-conscious logic of the dream.

C.B. But surely a play like *The Shepherd's Chameleon* is both conscious and critical?

E.I. Yes, I've written conscious and critical plays as well. 'Conscious' in inverted commas, because everything is either conscious or else unconscious in a special way. Sunlight, moonlight. There's daytime consciousness and night-time consciousness; daytime unconsciousness is a sort of oblivion. There are parallel levels of consciousness and awareness. *Rhinoceros*, for example.

C.B. Wasn't that play based on a nightmare?

E.I. Yes, it was partly a nightmare, a distant, assimilated nightmare. Which means it wasn't really a nightmare any more, it was something I had thought about quite coolly. I've been criticized not for saying in *Rhinoceros* that totalitarianism and collectivization are evil, but for not offering a solution. But I never meant to offer a solution. I simply meant to show how a mutation is possible in collective thought, to show how it comes about. I was quite simply, phenomenologically, describing the process of collective transformation. I was doing it in a completely lucid way, yet basing it upon my nightmare image. But I was no longer inside the nightmare, whereas when I was writing *Victims of Duty* or

How to Get Rid of It, I was in a nightmare state or at least in a state of astonishment. By a state of astonishment I mean that state of mind in which one level of consciousness is shattered, and another level appears or is in the process of appearing or hasn't yet appeared. People will tell me 'You just put down what comes into your head, you're not a lucid writer', but one shouldn't be allowed to say a thing *is*, at a time when as yet it isn't, when it's only just emerging. The play doesn't exist until I've written the word 'Curtain'. Plays like *The Bald Prima Donna*, *Victims of Duty* or *The Chairs* grew like trees as I wrote them: trees growing neither with the willpower of ordinary consciousness nor in defiance of it, growing without taking into account the consciousness which is there and which observes their growth. Consciousness *does* register, you're not completely stupid when you're writing.

C.B.   Is this presence of consciousness, which one could compare to a nightlight, reflected in the form of corrections, crossings out?

E.I.   I cross things out when I'm writing an article on Brancusi, or Gérard Schneider, or Byzantios, when I'm writing an article about my own plays, or about literature or poetic creation. When I'm writing plays, I don't really cross out at all. It's a different mental process entirely. I allow my mind a freedom that I don't allow it when I'm writing an article where things need to be logically linked, where the language has to be clear and coherent. But with poetry or plays, you have to prevent discursive thought from intervening.

C.B.   *Victims of Duty* has a nightmare, a series of images as its starting-point. But in *The Bald Prima Donna*, which you say you wrote in a similar state, wasn't it language rather than imagery that you allowed to take control? Wasn't the latter play essentially a question of the written word, and the former more a question of experience?

E.I. You can't really separate them. I've already said that when I write, I try to prevent discursive thought or daytime consciousness from creeping in, that I allow images to surface as freely as possible: but it can never be completely free. Conscious thought is always interfering and stopping the images from surfacing spontaneously; and it's equally true that even in discursive thought there are a number of repressed, unconscious thoughts. . . .

C.B. Are there moments when you get carried away by one element rather than another, by a memory or an image or by the idea you have of a character or by the language moving off mechanically of its own accord, one phrase leading automatically to the next? Or do they all get mixed up together?

E.I. Everything's mixed together, crowding in on me, offering itself—literary reminiscences, dreams, ideological polemic, an amazement at being, spontaneity, reflection, metaphysics, platitudes. . . . For instance, when I wrote *The Chairs*, I first had the image of chairs, then that of a person bringing chairs as fast as possible on to an empty stage. So I had this initial image but I didn't know at all what it meant. Later, I understood. In any case, I understood it a little sooner than the critics who said: 'This play is the story of two failures. Their life, and life in general, is failure, and absurdity. These two old people—who've never managed to achieve anything, who imagine that they're receiving guests—they think they exist, they try to delude themselves, to persuade themselves that they actually have something to say . . .'. In other words, the critics and spectators simply described the play's subject matter. But that wasn't really the point of the play. It was something quite different: it was the chairs themselves, and what the chairs meant—well, I've tried to under-

72

stand it, but it's like trying to interpret one's own dreams. I've said to myself: That's it, it's absence, emptiness, nothingness. The chairs remain empty because there's no one there. And at the end, the curtain falls to the accompanying noises of a crowd, while all there is on the stage is empty chairs, curtains fluttering in the wind, etc. . . . and there's nothing. The world doesn't really exist. The subject of the play was nothingness, not failure. It was total absence: chairs without people. The world does not exist because in the future it will stop being, everything dies, you know. Now people have given a clear, reasonable psychological explanation of the play, but what's there is another level of consciousness, an awareness of evanescence.

C.B. Wasn't writing the play just a question of elucidating this image of the empty chair?

E.I. I could write another play about what this play is; but the play itself consisted of empty chairs, and more chairs arriving, a whirlwind of them being brought on and taking over the whole stage as if a massive, all-invading void were settling in. . . .

C.B. The multiplication of the chairs.

E.I. It was both multiplication and absence, proliferation and nothingness.

C.B. By having the chairs proliferate, you extend this absence over the entire space of the stage, which represents all the space in the world.

E.I. Yes, that's it, all the space in the world.

C.B. I'm going to go back to my initial question. When you write a play, do you always start from either a dream or a conscious thought? And secondly, once you've chosen or

73

been given this starting point, how do you set about your work?

E.I. It varies quite a bit. As I've told you, I sometimes start with a short story, which is how *The Colonel's Photograph* became *The Killer*, sometimes from a dream or a remark, an idea, an image. For *Amédée or How to Get Rid of It*, the starting point was a dream I had of a corpse stretched out in a long corridor in a house I was living in. In *Jacques or Obedience* there are several dreams, one of a stallion galloping and catching fire—which I transposed with the greatest possible fidelity in the play—the dream of the little guinea pig, of little animals in a bath full of water and who stayed on the bottom without getting drowned. We have already talked about the dream of flying, which I've had several times and which was the starting point for my short story, *The Stroller in the Air*. And in my latest play too, *Hunger and Thirst*, there are several dreams: the dream about the woman in the flames, the dream about some member of the family, a dead person, whom I saw again after a long absence, very strangely dressed—I knew in my dream that this person was dead and I was surprised to be visited by him. And the dream about the cellar in the first act is one I have quite often: the dream about a house caving in. Somehow, it's the tomb; it's a dream my mother often appears in. That might be quite significant to a psychologist.

C.B. This is a theme that often appears in your work and that you've already talked about—the theme of foundering, sinking into the mud, being deprived of light.

E.I. That's right. In other plays, I start quite simply from a state of mind, a state of astonishment, a feeling that the world is strange. This was the case with *The Bald Prima Donna*. The play I wrote turned out to be a comic one although the original feeling was not a comic feeling. Several things grafted themselves on to this original starting point: the feeling of how strange the world was, people speaking a language I could no longer understand, ideas becoming emptied of their content, gestures stripped of meaning; and also a parody of the theatre, a criticism of the clichés of conversation. Basically, it's always the same. A play isn't this or that. It's several things at once, it's *both* this *and* that.

C.B.   How do you work? Do you need a timetable, an exact framework, any external stimuli?

E.I.   It varies a good deal. I have no set rules, no methods. It depends how I'm feeling, sometimes I write and sometimes I dictate. There are times when I regain a kind of calm and then I work every morning from nine to twelve, from nine to one. After all, writing isn't really work. . . . Personally, I regard existence as a misfortune. And I think it would be an even greater misfortune not to exist. But among the people who do exist, I'm really one of the most fortunate. I am more fortunate than kings because even kings work, whereas I can go where I like, when I like, with just a pencil and notebook; I don't have to clock in (I've had to in the past, and I know what it's like). So I get the feeling I'm a sulky child, that I'm thoroughly ill-tempered, that it's not at all nice of me to be so dissatisfied. At a time when some people are fighting wars and killing one another, when some are dying of hunger and others working hard for a living, I'm actually alive. Of course you could say that I don't work and you could say that I do. Both are equally true. I don't work since I can, on the face of it, do whatever I want, yet at the same time I'm a slave to words, to writing—and writing is really an agonizing business. Indeed if I do write, it's because of this feeling of guilt, for I am naturally inclined not to write, not to make any strenuous effort, in fact inclined not to work. It takes months on end for me to accumulate what I need for a single month's work. And what is there in the long months when I'm not working?

There's the desire to work, the gloom of not working, the fear of wasting my life—as if writing were a means of not wasting it—the thought that people are actually dying of hunger or being massacred while I'm strolling around Montparnasse. At any rate, all these forms of remorse build up a kind of accumulation of energy, and after several months I manage to amass enough energy for one month. I have to finish a play within a month or two because if it goes on any longer, it's hopeless, the end of the play may be ruined because I don't have any energy left.

C.B. And when you're working, how many hours a day do you work?

E.I. An hour, an hour and a quarter, an hour and a half, maybe two hours a day. Sometimes I even work for as long as four hours, but that isn't real work, because for some of the time I just write letters.

C.B. And how do you spend the rest of the day?

E.I. I relax.

C.B. Do you think about your play at the same time?

E.I. Yes, I do. Then I really relax, I do crosswords because crosswords allow you to think of quite different things . . . or of nothing at all.

C.B. Does writing the play free you of the guilt you feel in the periods when you're not working?

E.I. The idea of guilt can't be eradicated by creation. When I'm writing I still feel guilty, because I'm doing something that is really very vain and quite useless to fifteen hundred million human beings.

C.B. Haven't some of your characters, for instance Choubert in *Victims of Duty*, Amédée, or even Jean in *Hunger and Thirst*, inherited this feeling of guilt?

E.I. It's not the same guilt at all.

C.B. Doesn't a play like *Rhinoceros* imply an extension from the idea of individual guilt to the idea of collective guilt?

E.I. Guilt is not a collective feeling. A mob that runs riot, a lynch mob, doesn't feel guilty. The individual alone reflects and is capable of feeling or not feeling guilt.

C.B. I asked you just now if the fact of writing freed you from your feeling of guilt. You replied: 'No, it's when I write that I feel most guilty of all.' But would you write at all without this feeling of guilt?

E.I. People talk too much about guilt. Probably everything we've been saying about it is three-quarters wrong. I too am a victim of accepted clichés. It might be more apt to say that I write out of anguish; out of nostalgia . . . a nostalgia which no longer knows its object; or which, when it does settle on an object, realizes that its cause lies elsewhere. But where?

As far as guilt is concerned, why should I feel guilty? It's all right to feel pity, to regret that one can't save humanity . . . but I haven't done the world any harm. Let the jailers, the judges and the tyrants, the violent, the cynical and the deaf feel guilty first . . . then, I can decide whether I shall.

77

Claude Bonnefoy. You told me, in our last conversation, that you sometimes wrote and sometimes dictated your plays. Do the rhythms of writing and dictating seem fairly similar to you, or do they correspond to different needs?

Eugène Ionesco. When I write, the text tends to be more introspective. When I dictate, obviously it's more colloquial. *Exit the King* is a play which was dictated, and which did not—by the way—originate in a dream or in a state of free-ranging imagination. It is a very wide-awake play, very aware. Which means that the writing is much more consciously composed. People immediately said: 'Oh! he's given up the *avant-garde*, he's turning classical!' It wasn't a question of choosing between classicism and the *avant-garde*. I had quite simply written in a different style because I was on a different level of consciousness. Writing depends on the state of mind one's in.

C.B. What had your starting point been?

E.I. A feeling of anguish. This anguish was very simple, very clear. I had felt it in a less irrational, less visceral way—in other words, it was more logical, more conscious—logic is the surface level of consciousness. Dreams are deep, substantial consciousness. *Exit the King* was written in twenty days. I wrote first of all for ten days. I had just been ill and I'd been very scared. Then, after these ten days, I had a relapse and was ill for another fortnight. And at the end of the fortnight, I started writing again. I finished the play in the next ten days. Only I realized, on re-reading the play, and again when I saw it on the stage, that the first half had a rhythm that was no longer the same in the second half. There was a different rhythm, a different tempo, as if two separate pieces had been glued together. There was a distinct break in the middle of the play.

C.B. Did your illness have anything to do with your choice of subject?

E.I. Yes. That is to say it was my illness which induced me to write this play. I'd been meaning to write it for years, but I'd kept putting it off.

C.B. At the beginning of our conversations, you told me that when you were a child, you'd thought that if one was very careful, one would never die. This idea recurs in the second half of *Exit the King*, when the king says: 'I could decide not to die.' Would it therefore be true to say that this is a very old idea of yours, dating back to your childhood, which you rediscovered as a result of your illness?

E.I. Yes, I suppose so. To my memories of childhood, but not to my dreams. But there's something else besides: I told myself that one could learn to die, that I could learn to die, that one can also help other people to die. This seems to me to be the most important thing we can do, since we're all of us dying men who refuse to die. This play is an attempt at an apprenticeship in dying.

C.B. Do you think that writing it helped you?

E.I. It didn't help *me* at all. It may have helped other people, for instance the Rumanian translator of the play, a great poet, Ion Vinea. He was an old man and seriously ill when he decided to translate the play. He worked on it for three or four months. During these months he was virtually in his death throes. He finished the manuscript of his translation four or five days before his death. If he wanted to do this translation at a time when he knew he was going to die, and if he was able to and so anxious to finish it, it's possible that the play helped him. And if by chance it did, then I would feel justified and would dare to think that literature is not entirely useless.

C.B. Isn't death, or rather the theme of anguish, of knowing one is dying, one of the main themes in your plays? I'm thinking less of the direct and almost commonplace expression of death, the murder victims in *The Killer*, the corpse in *Amédée* or the suicide of the two old people in *The Chairs*, than of the various transpositions or symbolizations of the theme: Choubert's sinking, the catastrophic other place discovered by Bérenger in *A Stroll in the Air*, the nothingness in *The Chairs*, the dislocation of speech in *The Bald Prima Donna*.

E.I. I think you're right.

C.B. When you're writing, and starting not from a short story, which gives you a structure, but from a dream, an image or a sense of anguish, do you know from the outset how the play is going to unfold?

E.I. Sometimes I do, sometimes I don't. With *The Bald Prima Donna*, for example, I didn't know, although the play was written for the theatre in separate scenes: scene I, scene II, scene III, etc. . . . . It was the first real play I'd written as an adult, and I was writing it the way I thought a play ought to be written (whereas now I don't cut up my plays into scenes). I also gave all the stage directions: the character sits down, stands up, sits down again, the doorbell rings, someone gets up to answer it, someone enters left, enters right. . . . But in spite of this, I didn't have a specific plan, it just made itself as I was writing. I didn't know exactly how I was going to arrive at the final dislocation of language, at a deterioration that I definitely had in mind. The same thing is true for *The Chairs*.

C.B. In *Notes and Counter-Notes* you say that *The Bald Prima Donna* had several possible endings, and that in fact it was on the stage, with the actors themselves, that you finally decided how the play should finish. And the ending one sees in stage productions is different from the one that's printed in some editions. Why are there two possible endings? Is it because the ending is unimportant, because the essential thing is what comes before it, the simultaneously amazing and ordinary way the characters behave?

E.I.   First of all there are technical reasons. It was impossible, after I'd written the play, to use the ending I'd wanted, because it would have required a lot more characters, machine guns, etc. It's equally true that *The Bald Prima Donna* doesn't need to have an ending, or that it can have several, because it's about heterogeneity. The strange and the unusual can quite well be expressed on the stage by the arrival of characters who have nothing to do with the other characters, or by anything else for that matter. Everything is contingent, therefore all endings are possible; however, I wanted to give a meaning to the play by having it begin all over again with two characters. In this way the end becomes a new beginning but, since there are two couples in the play, it begins the first time with the Smiths and the second time with the Martins, to suggest the interchangeable nature of the characters: the Smiths are the Martins and the Martins are the Smiths. They are characters emptied of all substance, of all psychological reality. They are characters who say absolutely anything, and what they say has absolutely no significance. That's the play, and that's what I wanted: what the characters say has no importance whatever. People have tried to provide psychological, sociological and realistic interpretations of this, they've seen the characters as caricatures of the petty bourgeoisie. Maybe. They are, a little. But only a little. We tend to reduce everything we find strange to our own experience, to the universe we know by heart, but in fact there are only puppets in *The Bald Prima Donna*.

C.B.   To come back to the problem of the play's ending. What strikes me is that in several of your plays—I'm thinking particularly of *The Bald Prima Donna*, *The Lesson*, *Victims of Duty* and *Hunger and Thirst*—the final exchanges have a mechanical character that emerges either through the repetition of a single phrase or even of single words, or else through the recitation of a series of numbers. Is this just a device or does it have a deeper significance?

E.I. You're a critic, you should know better than I do. . . . Actually, there's no reason why a play should end. One should be able to stop at any point, the same as cutting a ribbon. Since a work of art is a transposition of life, any ending is artificial.

C.B. Except in a play where everyone has died.

E.I. But 'life' continues, even if heroes don't . . . the theatre continues. The end will stop being artificial when we ourselves are dead. It's death that closes a life, a play, a work of art. Otherwise, there is no end. To find an end is to simplify the art of playwriting, and I can understand why Molière didn't always know how to end his plays. We only need an end because the audience has to go home to bed.

C.B. If the audience never got tired, we might imagine a sort of permanent theatre.

E.I. It does in fact exist. The curtain goes up on something that began long ago, it goes down because we have to leave, but behind the curtain things go on indefinitely. The construction of a play is artificial, with a beginning and an end. Really, a play should have a far more complex construction that would enable it to have no end, or no construction, at least not this sort of construction, a transposition of events. Something should be left open. It's true for real life. Why should it be different for art?

82

C.B. Yes, but when, for instance, at the beginning of *The Chairs* or *The Bald Prima Donna*, you didn't know where you were going to come out, you found this opening, this dynamic movement.

E.I. What I mean is: a work of art is a fragment of life that you perceive within the limits of its time and space; but this life runs on and continues elsewhere. With *The Chairs*, I had simply the image of an empty room gradually being filled by empty chairs. The chairs pouring in, faster and faster, constituted the central image, they expressed for me an ontological void, a sort of whirlwind of emptiness. On this initial image, on this first obsession, I grafted the story of an old couple who are themselves on the edge of nothingness, and who have had problems all their lives. But their story is intended merely to support the initial, fundamental image which gives the play its meaning.

C.B. Isn't it also symptomatic that your plays often contain old people or at least elderly or unappealing ones, and also couples who've been together for a long time and whose lives have been shaken by all sorts of minor dramas?

E.I. Well, *Amédée* is certainly about a couple. But for me the essential thing about the play, the key to it, is the corpse. Everything else is just padding, even though it may have a meaning of its own. I see the corpse as transgression, original sin. The growing corpse is time.

C.B. Of course, but this guilt is felt by Amédée, and the couple as they analyse it define themselves in relation to it at the same time. Now if this couple, who are no longer young lovers and who recur in several of your plays, were there simply to illustrate an image, their appearance would be nothing more than a facile expedient. Doesn't it correspond to something deeper?

E.I. The couple is the world itself, it's man and woman, Adam and Eve, the two halves of humanity who love one another, find one another, who are sick and tired of loving one another; who, in spite of everything, cannot not love one another, who cannot exist except together. The couple here aren't just a man and a woman, they might also be the whole of mankind, divided and trying to come together again, to become one.

C.B. So there are two levels, the very concrete level of everyday gestures, gossip and quarrels; and another symbolic level on which these particular, minutely described gestures take on universal, symbolic importance?

E.I. Yes, I hope so. The characters help me give a truth to the symbols because they are more or less 'real' characters, characters who seem to exist, people you seem to see every day, true characters, if you can have such a thing. So their ordinariness sets off or accentuates all that's not ordinary, all that's unusual, strange or symbolic. I'm using the word symbol in the sense of an image with a meaning.

C.B. So do the characters help you to clarify these symbols, these images which you take as starting points?

E.I. These characters act as a foil. I use them to highlight the fantastic side because if you set realism against the unreal, you obtain a contrast which is also a union; in other words, the realism makes it easier to bring out the fantastic aspect and vice versa. To some extent I was doing what a painter, Byzantios, has just done. Byzantios is an abstract painter. He had painted abstract paintings in rather the same way that I had written abstract plays, *The Bald Prima Donna* being more or less an abstract play. Then suddenly, in his last exhibition, he invented something new: there is in his latest pictures a moving, living background, with rays of light, vibrations—a whole abstract drama. In fact it's this background that's the real

84

picture. In front of this background, as if it were on a proscenium, he paints an artichoke, a tree, a water-lily, etc. . . . so that this real or realistic or pseudo-realistic object gives its truth, its strength to the abstract background of the painting. I think that this is more or less what I did spontaneously in *The Chairs*, where there is this movement, this abstract whirlwind of chairs, while the two old people act as the pivot for a pure construction, for the moving architecture that a play really is; similarly in *Amédée* where there's the real corpse and the two characters who seem to exist.

C.B. You said just now that, starting from an initial image, you often found yourself working without knowing where you were going. Have you sometimes felt that you'd run into a complete dead end?

E.I. Not known how to get out of it, you mean? In *Amédée or How to Get Rid of It* I think you can tell that I had some trouble there.

C.B. Where exactly?

E.I. From the moment that the corpse breaks on to the stage. The two characters are there, staring at it. And I got stuck staring at it too. I no longer had any idea how to get rid of this corpse. What ought I do with it? As the characters are there, no longer knowing what to do, they talk, they say anything that comes into their heads. From the second half of the second act, you can tell that I'm more or less treading water.

C.B. Were you conscious of this when you were writing?

E.I. Yes, of course. With *A Stroll in the Air*, since I wanted to make a play from something that was anti-theatrical, I found it difficult to break into the theatrical. But later it clicked, I 'found' what was needed for this play. I think.

C.B. When you get this feeling of being at a dead-end, do you put your text aside and wait for the creative mechanism to start moving again—the way one puts green fruit on straw to make it ripen; or do you try to struggle with it immediately, starting off on any available track, ready to cross it all out later and start again?

E.I. It's very variable. With *A Stroll in the Air* I went on fighting it. I had to finish the play.

C.B. Because the producer was waiting for it?

E.I. Yes, external pressure, if you like.

C.B. But which coincides, I think, with what you've already told me, about needing to finish your plays quickly. Can an external pressure be productive?

E.I. On the whole, no. Or rather, yes.

C.B. Are you subject to anguish or anxiety in times of pressure?

E.I. Oh yes! I say to myself, it's a nuisance having to finish this piece of work. I ought to work on it for three months, six months, a year. Why should I hurry? I say to myself: 'Next time I'll start working in plenty of time and there'll be no architectural faults, no faults in the construction'. But I wait until next year, and next year when the season's already approaching, I'm asked for the play I'm intending to write, whose subject is already in my head. And I write it; I know that, this way, it's never really finished. But after all, it is only literature. So it's good enough: most works of literature don't last for more than a year anyway.

C.B. Do you think that your plays will last?

E.I. There's simply no way of knowing. We don't know

86

what future generations will be like. If their sensibilities are in tune with mine, my plays may continue to mean something; if not, that will be the end of them. It takes a few decades for a work to become brilliant—when it's no longer written by the author, but rewritten by the generations who come after him. Perhaps they're the ones who really write the novels, plays and poems.

C.B. But you have to provide them with a starting-point.

E.I. Yes, we do that. But they choose whether or not to accept this starting-point. That's where the element of chance comes in. Is a work of art really a work of art or is it what others make of it, what they want to think of it, etc? It's a problem I'll leave you to resolve. My own thoughts on the subject are very contradictory.

C.B. To come back to the subject of literary criticism. You spoke just now of construction and architecture. Do you think the architecture of a play must be completely thought out in advance or—and this would seem to fit in with what you were saying about *The Chairs* or *Amédée*—do you think it should take shape as the work progresses?

E.I. It can be thought out. It can also develop while you're writing. Plays like *Rhinoceros*, *The New Tenant* or *The Lesson* are constructed along classical lines. They have an initial theme, a simple progression .So the construction is simple, it's a transposition, of a kind of breathing perhaps, the transposition of a rhythm, of a movement. There are several ways of constructing plays. There are classical constructions, Romantic constructions, baroque constructions, types of construction which don't look like constructions at all but which are constructions nonetheless. *Rhinoceros* and *The Lesson* were both constructed in advance, although they were very different types of construction. With *The Lesson* I wanted to describe an ascending curve, to start out quietly and build to the professor's crescendo of madness, then to a violent fall. *Rhinoceros* had the construction of a short story transposed for the stage; but it also had a dramatic progression, a proliferation; a trap snapping shut on someone.

C.B.   Some of your plays, *Jacques or Obedience*, *The Bald Prima Donna*, *Victims of Duty*, for instance, seem to break with all recognizable schemes of construction, whether classical or Romantic, and yet these plays do have a unity of tone, of mood. How do you arrive at this unity? What kind of secret construction do you use?

E.I.   A construction that's . . . natural . . . or spontaneous: a newborn child has a head and legs. And even if it's deformed, if it lives, it's an organism with a psychology of its own, a being . . . worthy of interest, worthy of existence. Aesthetics is no longer the science of the 'Beautiful'. It studies imaginary beings who are laden with real meanings.

Claude Bonnefoy. Until it's actually been performed, a play has a purely literary existence. Its theatrical value is as yet uncertain. It is only on the stage that it will take on its real dimensions, albeit at the risk of the author's intentions being betrayed by the producer or the actors. We can talk about these possible betrayals later on. For the moment, I'm thinking about a passage in *Notes and*

Counter-Notes where you describe your astonishment, your surprise when you saw your characters come to life for the first time under the direction of Nicolas Bataille.

Eugène Ionesco. Oh yes. The strangest thing in a very strange world is seeing that one has actually created characters. When I saw flesh and blood people learning my text, becoming the Fireman, becoming the Maid, the Smiths and the Martins, or later becoming the King or becoming the Queen or the Old Man or Semiramis, I found it really astounding. Even now, although I'm more used to it, I'm still astounded. It's utterly strange to see an imaginary world taking on a real existence, it's a sight that always fills me with a kind of anguish. It makes me feel a little as if I were usurping God's place.

C.B. Has this experience helped you at all as far as creation is concerned?

E.I. You mean, in the sense of technical knowledge?

C.B. To begin with.

E.I. No, I don't think so. On the contrary. By which I mean that when I wrote my first plays, there was no construction; or rather, there was, but it was a rhythm, something that moved forward. The play ended because it had reached a slack period; but though the play ended, the life of the play continued. But after the third, fourth or fifth play, because I was certain the next one was going to be performed, I found it increasingly difficult to write. I'd say to myself: 'No, you can't do that, that's not something you can do on the stage. Now how am I going to cope with this, because there's only a small stage, because we've got only four or five actors. . . .' Not only has it not helped me, it's actually restricted me.

C.B.   And you don't believe in those exquisite, blessed constraints that Valéry wrote about?

E.I.   Of course, one can never say that a thing is this or that. It's both good and bad at the same time. So that this feeling of constraint has hampered me and, at the same time, helped me just a little. If you've only got three or four actors at your disposal, it's interesting to do something for three or four characters.

C.B.   When for instance a producer commissions a play from you. . . .

E.I.   People don't commission plays from me. They just ask for them. For some years now I've been lucky enough to have friends who ran small theatres: Serreau, Marcel Cuvelier, Mauclair, Poliéri, and Postec, who together with Mauclair was possibly my best producer. Once they knew I was writing a play, they wanted it quickly. So I had to finish it.

C.B.   Did discussions with producers help you see what you might do more clearly?

E.I.   I don't think so. It's not very modest of me to say so, but I think that they found it rather difficult to follow me, to accept this theatre which, at the time, seemed somewhat barbaric. In most cases, I clashed with my producers. Especially in the beginning. The producers had a rather realistic vision of the theatre, an essentially logical turn of mind. Despite Dullin, Jouvet and Pitoëff, they hadn't moved very far from Antoine. In literature, painting and music there had been some amazing experiments: surrealism, Picasso's painting, non-figurative painting, the new music, etc. . . . Psychology had made enormous advances. The theatre was lagging behind. There was still a certain conventional realism in the theatre. The fault lies partly with the *théâtre de boulevard* which is still going strong, combining realism and entertainment; and partly with the educational theatre, the popular theatre. Because that's what the *théâtre de boulevard* is: the desire to please. We on the other hand are not worried about displeasing, about quite often offending the audience. Every work is either aggressive or else demagogic, commercial, an 'entertainment play'. Sometimes, instead of conquering the public by force, we can please them spontaneously. We don't do it on purpose. We don't like 'concessions'. Novelty means insolence. There is no life, no movement in art, without aggression, without novelty. Yes, aggression is novelty. Theatre people would have preferred either to amuse the bourgeoisie effortlessly, or else to educate them. It's a problem that we're still living with, but this desire to educate is beginning to disappear.

C.B. It seems to me to be still very much alive.

E.I. Certainly. Nonetheless, some *avant-garde* writers, really progressive ones, do want to break away from committed literature. Who do I mean by progressive? Not the English or French or Germans who are didactic, populist, dogmatic, blinkered fanatics; but the young Russian, Polish and Hungarian writers, who need freedom and who feel this need very deeply. Freedom is gulped down every day in Paris and the St.-Germain-des-Prés cafés, with rolls and coffee, or a glass of beer; here, it's so common that no one notices it; intellectuals from Eastern countries feel its absence and their need for it, they are hungry and thirsty for freedom; we are not living under a tyranny, the police don't arrest us all the time; it's the Eastern European poets who will give freedom a new virginity; who will make us understand it, who will make us understand that we really are free. Not entirely . . . we've got all sorts of freedom, but less freedom of mind, less imaginative power. Russian writers, the ones who haven't been completely sterilized and

91

stifled by academic realism and academic socialism, want freedom in the realms of the imagination, too.

Imagination isn't escape. Imagining is building, it's making, creating a world. . . . By first creating worlds one can 're-create' the real world in the image of the invented, imaginary worlds. You don't 'correct' the world, you 'erect' a new one. But to continue. I was saying that when I started having my plays performed, producers were surprised by the kind of thing I was doing. They liked it, but they were put out by it at the same time. How were they to translate this kind of theatre on to the stage? How could they have fifty chairs brought on to the stage? Sylvain Dhomme did it, Mauclair did it, the Germans didn't want to do it. They didn't understand. At first, for instance, I had the greatest difficulty in getting Serreau to allow me to keep the corpse's gigantic feet in *Amédée*. In effect, what you have in *Amédée* is a corpse that grows and grows until it takes up the whole flat. At first, it's in the next room. Then the moment comes when it's grown so big that it pushes through the door: you see its feet appear. The two people who've killed him, and who are standing in the dimly-lit dining-room, see the dead man growing before their very eyes like the pangs of remorse. I wanted feet that were five feet long. Serreau was dubious. He was going to order feet two foot six long. He thought even that was too big. We had a slight argument about it. I said that feet two and a half feet long were too close to normal size, that the effect would be pure *grand guignol*; for their appearance to be truly fantastic and not simply grotesque, we'd have to go well beyond normal proportions. Serreau was quite willing to get away from realism, but he didn't really dare go completely beyond it. To give the corpse feet five feet long seemed to him excessive; but he did it all the same in the end. Since then, Serreau has understood the whole thing much better; when he produced my plays again, I'm thinking particularly of the Odéon productions, he was far more imaginative about them than I was. For *Amédée* at the Odéon he really managed to abolish all dimensions. At the end, when the carachter flies off, he managed to make it extraordinarily festive. For instance, there was a sort of enormous luminous ball hanging from the flies, that spun round and sent little spots of light dancing all over the theatre; there were stars, all kinds of visual happenings, a merry-go-round of stars; this production of Serreau's was tremendous. Do people still remember it?

C.B. So to perform your plays, producers and actors had first to find a new style?

E.I. Yes. And if *The Bald Prima Donna* has been produced the way it has, if there isn't greater violence on the stage, if the characters aren't more disjointed, it's because the actors didn't dare to go all the way, or didn't feel the full force of it. They didn't think you could go that far in the theatre.

I'd written this play with detailed production notes; or at any rate, I'd plotted most of the moves. What had to be found was a particular way of acting it. And we finally found it. Or at least we found one, which was extremely interesting. I wanted to work up to a final explosion, but it wasn't possible. Moreover, as I've already said, I wanted this play to express the feeling of strangeness that the world inspires in me. The characters are completely emptied of their content; so are their words. For instance, you may say, or hear, the word 'horse'. You can understand the phrase, 'I'm getting on my horse'. But it's possible for the word to get emptied of its content, for you no longer to hear anything but the sound 'horse, horse, horse'. Sometimes it's not only the sound, it's all reality that's emptied of its content. You can find yourself looking at things that seem to be mere appearances, expressions of nothing, faces with nothing behind them. That's what I wanted to express in this play. Its actual performance turned it slightly into some-

93

thing else: a parody of the theatre, a series of gags, a new way of achieving comedy. . . .

The play was very well staged, the actors' performances were very interesting; they did in fact largely express what was supposed to be expressed. That dream-like state, that state of astonishment in the face of an increasingly disjunctive and dislocated reality—which was at the root of the linguistic comedy—was something I managed to bring out later in other plays, in *How to Get Rid of It*, with the swelling corpse which you see, then don't see, then which vanishes completely; in *Victims of Duty* with the climbing sequence; in *The New Tenant* with the furniture piling up around a character, completely hiding him until he's more or less buried under all the cupboards and chairs.

C.B. But all things considered, you get on well with your producers?

E.I. It's mainly abroad that there are problems. In France we work together; even if the result isn't entirely what I want, there's a sort of fusion that takes place between what *I* want and what *they* want. In the end, since we're working together, we no longer know exactly where we are, what *I* wanted and what *they* wanted; and something interesting comes out of this fusion.

C.B. Could you give me some examples of the problems you've had abroad?

E.I. In England when Peter Hall produced *The Lesson* in 1955, the new English theatre didn't yet exist. I think the impetus for it came from us. Later on English writers and producers did do something different; but without Beckett, Adamov, Weingarten, Tardieu, Ghelderode, myself, they might never have got started. . . .

The proof of this is that in 1955 Peter Hall, who was then a young producer—25 years old—and who was running a theatre, wanted to do something new. He already had one play he considered *avant-garde*: *Sacrifice to the Wind* by André Obey. He was looking for a second one. He'd heard about *The Lesson*. He'd read it in English because he couldn't read French. And he said to me: 'Yes, I'd be happy to produce this play, but we'd have to get another translator because this translation is no good. I don't believe you could possibly have written anything like this. The text is completely senseless, your translator hasn't understood a word of it.' I replied: 'It's the text that's stupid; I meant it to be.' So then he accepted it just the same. He agreed to produce it, but with one amendment. The professor kills forty pupils a day and the forty-first arrives. He's going to kill her too and the next day he'll begin all over again. Now this, Peter Hall said, was not possible. He was quite willing to accept that the professor could kill two pupils a day, that he could put them into a single coffin, that no one in the town would notice anything unusual. But forty students a day—that he couldn't accept. After a good deal of haggling I got him to agree that the professor could kill four a day. Four was possible, forty wasn't.

A similar thing happened with *Rhinoceros* in the United States. The producer found the subject of the play perfectly natural and plausible; he found it quite normal that a rhinoceros should be walking round the town, that a second rhinoceros should also be at large and wandering round, that someone should turn into a rhinoceros, that we should hear of ten people having been transformed, that everyone in the town should have turned into a rhinoceros. But there was one thing that worried him. He said to me: 'Look, if you don't mind, I'm going to write in an extra line of dialogue. Here's the reason. At the beginning of the third act Bérenger, the hero of the play, goes to visit his friend Jean. He knocks at the door and Jean asks: "Who is it?" Bérenger replies: "It's me, Bérenger." I hope you won't mind if I add a line at the end of the second act because

95

this opening just isn't possible. I'll have to do something to put it right.' 'What?', I asked him. 'Oh, it's easy,' he said, 'at the end of the second act there's a telephone in the office Bérenger's in. He can walk over, pick it up, and dial a number and say: "I'm going to phone my friend Jean to find out if he's in." Then after he's listened to it ringing for a bit he can add: "He's not answering. Perhaps the telephone is out of order. I guess I can go and visit him without telephoning first."' In other words, everything, even the improbable, seemed quite normal to this producer except the fact that someone might visit a friend without telephoning first.

C.B.　In a way he wanted to preserve realism, plausibility. I suppose the fantastic mustn't be allowed to destroy the conventions of American good manners.

E.I.　This same feeling for realism prevented the German productions of *The Chairs* from ever having any of the fantasy ballet aspect that the play should have. In Germany *The Chairs* has been performed often and very successfully; though in my opinion the German productions never really worked. The Germans absolutely refused to have fifty chairs brought on to the stage, as fast as possible. They also wanted the old woman to be played by an old woman so as to make it seem more real. Now this wouldn't do at all because her performance has to be a positive gymnastic feat, a real ballet with the chairs.

C.B.　How many chairs did you finally get?

E.I.　The producer Dugellin allowed me twelve chairs. He explained that the first person to arrive in the room was the invisible woman—so you need one chair—then the invisible colonel—a second chair—then other invisible people, to whom the two old people speak and who have to have chairs as well. After that people go on pouring in but there aren't any scenes to introduce them. So the producer felt that twelve chairs was as far as he could go. Now the important thing about the play is to create the sense of a crowd. If there are fifty chairs, you still have to give the impression that there are many more of them, that there's an enormous invisible crowd. If it's performed with only twelve chairs, all you're left with is the story of two old dotards who believe or pretend to believe that they're entertaining a few friends, etc., and the play is no longer what it ought to be, it no longer serves to illustrate its point.

C.B.   Well, so much for the disappointments. But is there no producer, or actor, or production that has taught you something new, revealed certain theatrical possibilities to you?

E.I.   Yes, Mauclair. With *Victims of Duty* he went well beyond a realistic vision, and with very simple means. In this play there's a character who climbs an invisible mountain. I didn't know how to put this across on the stage. Mauclair found a fantastic way of doing it. There was a table in the middle of the stage. Chauffard was making an imaginary journey. Among other things, he had to go through a forest. When he was doing this, he'd crawl under the table. Then he'd stand up, holding on to the table; at that moment, he'd be at the foot of the mountain. He'd climb on to the table. Someone would put a chair on top of it. This made the climb harder and steeper; he'd manage to climb on to the chair. He'd stay there for a bit, then he'd stand up on the chair; you really felt he was climbing a steep mountain. This is one of the fairly rare moments when I've understood what the theatre is, what it ought to be: a real, living experience, not just the illustration of a text. I'm not very fond of the theatre or plays and, when I read them, I never feel a need to go to the theatre and see them performed. But when I saw Chauffard climbing on to the table and from the table on to the

97

chair, it was something he was really experiencing and making the spectator experience too. That was a moment of real theatre because it was true and false at the same time.

If I see someone kill someone else, really kill him, it is a terrible, dramatic action, but one that's isolated in its very horror. Whereas we know quite well that art must be exemplary, something that signifies something else. With Chauffard it really was like that, as if one were experiencing the real meaning. I experienced a real theatrical moment then, not because of myself, but because of what Mauclair had brought to life.

C.B.   Have you had any other revelations of this kind?

E.I.   On the level of understanding, a critic, Morvan Lebesque, made me aware of the theme of proliferation in *Amédée or How to Get Rid of It* and some other plays. Previously, it was a theme I'd been using only half-consciously.

As far as productions are concerned. . . . Yes, there was great skill and a great deal of subtlety in Robert Postec's Brussels production of *Exit the King*. I've told you, I think, that there's a break, a change of tone in this play. In Paris people noticed it because, at a certain point, the play flagged, trying to get its second wind. When the king seems ready to die, he says, 'and if I decided not to die'. And Postec made the whole play spring to life again here; a second agony began. Here, in Paris, people got rather bored, and started complaining: 'Isn't it ever going to end?' They wanted to see the king dead and buried then and there. But Postec organized the whole thing very well. He understood that there were two movements, almost two plays. So when the king is ready to die, when everyone round him, the two queens, the doctor, the guard, Juliette is murmuring: 'You are going back home', etc. . . . round the throne, there is no light on the stage. And suddenly when the king says, 'if I decided not to die', Postec makes him say it not as an impotent, dying man who's clinging to life, but very forcefully and violently, as if the king really could decide not to die; the whole stage is then lit up again, the characters around the king run to the four corners of the stage to take up their original positions, the ones they had at the beginning of the play. In this way Robert Postec gave the audience the feeling that something new was beginning, a new death agony, a new departure, another adventure, a new play. You no longer had a feeling of slackening, of a change of rhythm, because Postec has *accentuated* the break instead of trying to hide it.

C.B. I want to go back to non-realism. What, according to you, is the best way of suggesting the unexpected, the fantastic on the stage? Is it through the actor's performance, as it was with Mauclair and Chauffard in *Victims of Duty*? Or is it through recourse to mechanical props and stage effects as you did with Barrault in *A Stroll in the Air*?

E.I. I received a lot of criticism over those mechanical tricks. Why shouldn't you use theatrical machinery? In the seventeenth and eighteenth centuries there were *pièces à machinerie* with flying chariots and gods coming down from heaven. Brecht too used this kind of thing in *The Good Woman of Setzuan* but no one criticized him for that. Even if they are an easy way out artistically, machines are fun and I don't see why I shouldn't use them. Though it's true that, for *The Chairs* and *Victims of Duty*, Sylvain Dhomme and Mauclair created the fantastic without stage effects—created something entirely inward.

C.B. Your theatre is essentially oneiric in inspiration. This inspiration presupposes images, some of which can be very complex and spectacular. Don't you sometimes need machinery to transpose them to the stage, to make them accessible to the audience?

E.I. Sometimes machinery is useful, possibly even indispensable, and sometimes not. When you're using these technical means, it's not the stuff of dreams you're creating, but rather the stuff of fantasy or humour. When you do this, what interests people is the ingenuity of it. In *A Stroll in the Air*, when Jean-Louis Barrault started to fly, people laughed because they knew there was some trick to it. They didn't know what, because the apparatus was very well disguised. There are far simpler ways of creating dreams, even though one doesn't always know what they are. I think that the actors have to act in a completely natural way and that there should be something that provides a particular atmosphere, an object whose presence causes unease or which is the personification of danger as in Boris Vian's *Les Bâtisseurs d'Empire*. Similarly in one of Weingarten's plays there are completely realistic characters who quarrel and abuse one another for financial reasons. In these scenes where the characters are speaking quite naturally, somewhere on the stage there's a black bird, a bird of death; its presence gives the play a completely different tone, the atmosphere of a real dream. People have in fact noticed that dreams are realistic. In the old days they'd try to create a dream atmosphere in the theatre by using gauze curtains and improbable, ghost-like characters.

C.B. That was the tradition of Maeterlinck and the Symbolists.

E.I. Yes, but people who are dreaming don't know they're dreaming.

C.B. And in Weingarten's play, the black bird is what shows that it is a dream, what sets it apart from reality. In the theatre, this sign can perfectly well be hidden in a corner.

E.I. What one needs is for there to be some inexplicable object. With *A Stroll in the Air* I didn't want to write a dream play, to convey a feeling of anguish (for anguish is what best expresses the dream). The play was really about a game, an obvious game, which explains why I used theatrical machinery. There were just a few dramatic, nightmare scenes: Josephine's dreams.

C.B. When do you think the author is in most danger of being betrayed? Is it when he writes a dream-like play that requires very simple signs which can, if necessary, be conveyed by a simple gesture; or is it when he writes a fantastic work that requires all kinds of mechanical props?

E.I. One has fewer worries with machinery. The problems are simple. The machines have to be technically perfect, and that's it. It's far more difficult to create a dream mood, a mood of unreality, of surreality, of deep anguish, and it requires far greater subtlety because it all hinges upon very little, a gesture, or some object that's both banal and strange.

C.B. I am thinking now of Roberta's three-nosed mask in *Jacques or Obedience*. Is this the disturbing object, the symbol of the dream-world? Is it a variation on the theme of proliferation? Noses multiplying here like cups and chairs elsewhere? Or is it simply a theatrical mask, an elementary theatrical prop?

E.I. Obviously it's a mask. Perhaps no one has looked hard enough, but so far they haven't found an actress who really has three noses! I was thinking here of certain Mesopotamian goddesses of agriculture who represent the earth and therefore fertility and sexuality. The dream aspect was mainly in the text of what Roberta says and in Jacques' behaviour as he begins to run around the three-nosed bride, becoming a horse, and then a stallion.

C.B. Metamorphosis is another problem. Jacques is transformed into a horse. All the characters in *Rhinoceros* apart from Bérenger become rhinoceroses. How do you conceive, and how do the producers and actors conceive, this metamorphosis taking place? Hasn't this caused some problems?

E.I.   There are several ways of conceiving metamorphosis. Barrault and also the Germans showed rhinoceroses on the stage. I had suggested a simple theatrical trick: having the character who was being transformed go into an adjoining room. From his room he could go into the bathroom, offstage, and reappear with a horn. Since it was morning and he'd be getting washed and dressed, he could move between the stage (his bedroom) and the wings (the bathroom); each time he reappeared his horn would be bigger, his skin greener, etc. . . . Those were the mechanical means. Other producers in Switzerland, the U.S. and Rumania didn't use either these masks or any accessories. They preferred to achieve an inner transformation. It's far more difficult, but when this 'moral' transformation is successful it can be very disturbing. The odd thing is that when you don't use any props, the play becomes blacker, more tragic; when you do use them, it's comic, people laugh. Jean-Louis Barrault chose the comic way because he thinks that in France the most tragic plays are the most comic: he'll cite *Tartuffe*, *The Misanthrope*, *The Miser*. It's a way of understanding the tragic and of putting it across.

C.B.   It seemed to me that, without props, the Rumanians managed to convey very convincingly the change from humanity to animality. The mechanical aspect of collective psychology was very well brought out. With Barrault it was this aspect that was most superficial, prettier.

E.I.   Yes, though it did enable Barrault to achieve more of a progression. It started out as comedy, when you saw the

102

first rhinoceros, and then afterwards, when certain characters like Botard were transformed, you no longer actually saw the transformation but just imagined it, and this was far more disturbing. I think that without the intial comedy, the play might have become harsh, unbearable. Perhaps Barrault was afraid . . . of his public.

C.B.   Has an actor ever revealed certain aspects of a character to you?

E.I.   Yes, one example of this was a Swiss actor who played in *The Lesson* in Lausanne. He was a rheumaticky little fellow, with a slight stoop, and he played the professor; his partner, the pupil, was a strapping young girl. The production was very interesting. Projectors threw the shadows of the two characters on to the wall and it was most impressive, particularly when the situation was reversed and you saw this sturdy girl being finally sucked dry by the spider of a teacher. It wasn't just rape, it was vampirism.

C.B.   And you hadn't thought of vampirism when you were writing the play?

E.I.   No. I had actually to see it acted. It was obvious. As the action progressed, he was devouring the girl, drinking her blood. And as he became stronger, her life was being sapped away, until in the end she was nothing but a limp rag.

C.B.   Do you think that revelations of this kind, whether provided by a producer or an actor, can be of use to an author?

E.I.   Yes, I must admit it. You're making me contradict myself. Which proves that no statement can be absolute.

Themes

Claude Bonnefoy. Eugène Ionesco, in most of your plays the mechanical aspect is very important. Moreover, it assumes different forms in different plays, and sometimes these different forms can be combined within a single play: there's the mechanical nature of language, the automatism of behaviour, the proliferation of objects, the acceleration and chaotic disintegration of the action. But that's not all. The very way you use these mechanisms constitutes a break with the mechanics of traditional drama. In the classical theatre there are two basic dramatic mechanisms: a tragic mechanism which corresponds to the fate that leads the hero to his death; and a comic mechanism which involves the repetition of phrases or situations, the tangling up of the plot which must then be unravelled all at once (there's a parallel here with the suspense of serious drama), and finally the speeding up of the action. But usually these mechanisms are extraneous to the characters, they constitute a mesh or several meshes which the characters cannot escape. On the one side you have fate, on the other the tripwire to make the clown fall down. In your work, on the other hand, the mechanical aspect starts out as something comic and ludicrous that appears to derive from the actual behaviour of the characters; it gradually increases, until suddenly, because of its very excessiveness or the fact that it's quite out of control, it becomes tragic. The finest illustration of this transition from the ludicrous to the tragic is in the script of *Anger* which you wrote for Sylvain Dhomme. What importance do you attach to this mechanism and to this transition from comic to tragic?

Eugène Ionesco. You're helping me see certain things more clearly. I realize now that this isn't just a formula or a dramatic device. It's a mode of being. At the start, you have 'a little of something mechanical encrusted on the living'. It's comic. But if the mechanical gets bigger and bigger and the living shrinks and shrinks, things become stifling and then tragic, because we get the impression that the world is slipping from our mental grasp. I had this same agonizing feeling, I think I've already mentioned it, when reading certain plays by Feydeau. The sorcerer's apprentice must have had this same anguished feeling of the world escaping his grasp. Perhaps it's also the image of what could happen in the near future. We are, now, no longer masters of the extraordinary machines we set in motion. Our planet could go up in smoke . . . so they tell us.

C.B. This loss of control is tragic, isn't it, because of its very logic, like the thought processes of psychiatric patients which are connected by a rigorous logic but based on a false premise which is itself the sign of a break with reality?

E.I. I have the feeling that the world too could start running haywire, like a machine. In *Anger*, it's the world which goes mad, which explodes, carried away by our passions. Passion has a mechanism which goes beyond its own aims. For instance people have strikes, riots or revolutions to obtain very specific results. In the heat of passion they may well go beyond their original goal, and end by installing a new tyranny, by setting up domestic stupidity, organized collective murder, and so on. It's as though at a certain point they lose control of themselves, and go mad. And something that should have been good turns out bad. Revolution becomes regression; freedom becomes alienation; administration, a loathsome abuse of power; justice, unbridled sadism; and so on.

C.B. In *Anger* the disorder begins quite flatly with some minor everyday incidents which disrupt the amicable relations between husband and wife, between friends. . . .

E.I. Yes, a whole variety of irrational outbursts, the whole mechanism of hatred, can crystallize around a trivial dissatisfaction.

C.B. An interesting thing about your plays is that one finds this mechanism in very different forms, so different in fact that one does not always recognize it immediately. . . .

E.I. Where did you find it? It'll take me a moment to think of it myself. Firstly, in *The Bald Prima Donna*. At a certain point, it's as though someone had flipped a switch that made the whole conversation go off the rails, made everything go haywire. In *The Chairs*, it's in the form of acceleration, this ballet of chairs that Semiramis brings on to the stage at an ever-increasing rate. In *Amédée*, it's again acceleration, with the corpse growing in a geometric progression. In *The New Tenant*, the removal men bring in the furniture more and more rapidly and it ends up suffocating the owner.

C.B. Here one can see a relationship between the theme of invasion in *The New Tenant* and the theme of being sucked down that one finds in *Victims of Duty*. They most probably have a common root in the obsession of the world being torn in two, the idea of a world where man is constantly assaulted by nature, by his own language, in other words by uncontrollable mechanisms which more often than not he himself has set in motion.

E.I.   It's words that proliferate in *The Lesson*.

C.B.   Words, and murder.

E.I.   And murder, that's true. In *Rhinoceros*, it's those pachyderms that proliferate. And someone, Bérenger, is surrounded, assaulted. He's left alone among the rhinoceroses just as the 'new tenant' is left alone in an encroaching and hostile world. It's the same thing really. Beyond the obvious theme, with its obvious sociological implications, there are psychological implications that are less obvious.

C.B.   In *Rhinoceros*, for instance, the drama of solitude, of individuality, of conscience faced with the workings of society.

E.I.   Should I try to say what particular anguish this reflects, where this fear comes from? Is it the fear of uncontrollable forces getting the upper hand, of everything suddenly exploding? Is it the dread of madness?

C.B.   Isn't the mechanism rooted in the automatism of dreams?

E.I.   I don't think so. The illogicality of dreams (which conceals another sort of logic) is quite different from the illogicality of the machine running wild, which as you said just now is not strictly speaking illogical at all, but rather a logic pushed to its limits.

C.B.   In *Notes and Counter-Notes*, in connection with *The Bald Prima Donna*, you talk of an 'attempt to make the mechanics of the theatre function in a vacuum'.

E.I.   There's nothing dreamlike about that play. The movements of a dream, the associations of images, are completely different. There is no rigorous progression in a dream. You go from one image to another, the associations are quite free. They appear to be more disorderly; in fact in a very natural way they are obliged to follow a certain movement of the soul, of the individual being. Dreams are natural, they are not insane. It is logic that is in danger of becoming insane; dreams, since they are the very expression of life in all its complexity and incoherence, cannot be mad. But logic can be. So can ideological systematology, which makes the relative absolute and tries to make an objective reality out of subjectivity.

C.B. That must be why you have a logician in *Rhinoceros*, a logician who soon founders in the general madness.

E.I. Obviously logic is outside of life. In logic, in dialectics, in systematologies, all the mechanisms come into play, all types of madness are possible: it is well-known that systematologies lose touch with reality.

C.B. It seems to me that in your plays the mechanism is both a theatrical device and a non-device at the same time, in so far as you use the theatre and its traditional devices to reveal mechanisms which are not the artificial mechanisms used in the *théâtre de boulevard*, but real ones: the mechanisms of behaviour, of language, and so on.

E.I. There's mechanical behaviour, an absence of life and therefore of thought, and there's mechanical language. ...

C.B. Hence the rejection of psychology—at least in the sense that teachers of literature use the word—which characterizes some of your plays.

E.I. This is probably where the ludicrous side of the characters, their lunatic side, stems from. Madness is being separated from oneself, it's being out of tune with reality. There are characters who dream, and others who are incapable of dreaming.

III

Those who don't dream are mad; because they dream just the same, they dream when they're awake, which is when they shouldn't.

C.B. It seems to me that your plays are built on a strange antithesis, not always noticeable within a single play but quite plain if one considers your work as a whole. On the one hand, there's the mechanical, the non-psychological, everything connected with automatic behaviour, or language running riot. On the other, there's psychoanalysis, dreams, anguish, obsessions. And one can't help wondering whether your interest in the mechanical is not connected with the fact that you are deeply affected by dreams, by your inner life. The mechanical, at once fascinating and disturbing, is what threatens the inner life, just as the rhythm of life itself or the ideas imposed by society paralyse or dam up spontaneity.

E.I. You've defined my attempts better than I could have done it myself. In theatrical terms, this antithesis is that of comedy and tragedy.

C.B. Why, since you attribute so much importance to dreams and hence to the tragic aspect of life, did you begin by writing a play, *The Bald Prima Donna*, where the mechanical and the comic dominate, at least superficially?

E.I. Because this mechanical theatre was what was most alien to me. Even in *The Bald Prima Donna*, the comic isn't as comic as all that. It is comic for other people. Basically, it's the expression of a type of anguish. And the comic is the start of the tragic, isn't it? One simply speeds up the movement for comedy; and slows it down for tragedy.

C.B. You began with what was most alien to you. Can one then take it that your true personality emerged only in your later plays?

E.I. In my first plays I was moving cautiously. Or I was denouncing the mechanical: rationalism leads to madness. The man whose mind feeds on dreams may re-discover the archetypes; in any event, he isn't imprisoned by clichés. The archetype is not the stereotype.

C.B. People have talked a lot about the absence of communication in connection with your plays, particularly the early ones. They've described your characters as people who were trying to understand one another but without succeeding, people who were deaf to what other people had to say to them and who therefore were simply talking in a vacuum. Now you've told me that *The Bald Prima Donna* was not about the failure to communicate. I should like to go into this in rather more detail. Is your theatre one of non-communication or not?

E.I. I think not. Some years ago, it was fashionable to talk about the failure to communicate. And about solitude, and about absurdity. These were fashionable words in 1950, in the way 'authenticity' and 'experience' were before 1940. No, I don't believe in non-communication. There's no such thing. There is also a lot of talk about a crisis of language. But this crisis is always deliberately whipped up by someone, by propagandists for instance. When Hitler said, 'The Czechs are going to attack me, I'm only attacking them to defend myself', he was deliberately creating confusion. When people say, 'The Americans attacked in Korea', it's simply not true; it was the Chinese. People will then explain that the Americans could have attacked, that if they didn't attack militarily they attacked theoretically. Once the word 'theoretically' has been brought into the discussion you arrive at the statement: 'They were the attackers.' I'm not discussing a line of thought or talking about taking sides, I am simply remarking that it is quite possible—deliberately—to deflect language from its normal course. As far as the characters in my first play are concerned, they don't want to communicate, they have no desire to. They are emptied of all psychology. They're simply mechanisms. And being mechanisms, if they are unable to communicate it is merely with themselves. They don't think. They are separated from themselves. They inhabit the world of the impersonal, the world of the collective. They live in a collectivist society which one cannot interpret simply as being the communist collectivist society, since capitalist bourgeois society is also collectivist. In short, the characters in my plays are people who pronounce slogans to save themselves the trouble of thinking. If I really believed absolutely that communication was impossible, I wouldn't write. An author is by definition someone who has faith in words.

I believe communication is possible, except when people resist it for a variety of different reasons: intellectual dishonesty, lack of attention, political involvement, temporary incomprehension. It can also fail to take place because of a lack of initiation into certain techniques, skills, terminologies, culture. Such difficulties can be lessened and even be made to disappear with a bit of intensive 'culturization'. The important thing at first is to define one's terms. That was what we were taught to do in our first year as philosophy students. Nowadays people no longer define their terms from the outset. There's also, of course, the fact that systems of expression aren't always designed for communicating, they are often used to conceal ideas. Ideologies are generally alibis, they intentionally conceal things that are quite different from the ones they admit.

C.B. If people labelled your work as the theatre of non-communication, wasn't this because, at the time, communication between yourself and either the public or the critics was very shakily established?

E.I. Communication may not be impossible, but it can sometimes be difficult. People were probably just not making the necessary effort to understand the kind of theatre I and several other writers were trying to create at that time. Probably because they were used to an entirely different verbal system. Although what we were trying to do was in fact extremely simple.

C.B. You didn't share the same system of communication.

E.I. Yes. If they'd wanted to, they could have understood what it was all about right from the beginning. Drama criticism, except in the case of a few individuals whom I shan't mention by name so as to spare their modesty, was and is a kind of second-class literary criticism. Since the nineteenth century drama criticism has been inferior to literary criticism, to art criticism, to philosophical thought. This inferiority is the result of journalistic impressionism, the desire to sound sophisticated—the fact that a newspaper critic always feels himself obliged to crack a joke, to be 'witty'. The result is absolutely witless. Drama criticism has inherited the mentality of the *théâtre de boulevard*. A *pièce de boulevard* was not a serious affair, still less a distressing one.

C.B. Whereas the comic theatre of the fifties dealt with really fundamental problems.

E.I. At any rate it tried to. The comic plays of the so-called 'theatre of the absurd'—I use the word because I can't think of another at the moment—are a little more serious than the *drames de boulevard*.

C.B. People also said that your characters were solitary, cut off from the world, this solitude being the corollary of their inability to communicate. Is there, so far as they are concerned, a drama of solitude?

E.I. No. As I think I've already said, people have a deep need for solitude. The lack of solitude is one of the main things

115

wrong with the modern world. What is the greatest discomfort in certain socialist countries where there's an acute housing shortage? It's being forced to share a flat with several other people. It makes people nervous, it leads to denunciations. Let's take an everyday example. You get on a bus at the second stop on the route. The seat near the driver is already taken. Why? Because it's a single seat. Everyone wants to be alone, so everyone has his eye on this single seat. The same thing happens in the Underground. What does a working person look for? A small quiet corner. Solitude is a need, everyone avoids everyone else. Dostoyevsky said long ago that if you spend three days with a person you love, at the end of those three days that person will have become your worst enemy.

There is such a thing as communal solitude. That's the bad kind. Real solitude is not so much isolation as a withdrawal into oneself. It is when I have this kind of solitude that I am really at one both with myself and with other people, who are no longer irritating, whose presence has been purified and become purely spiritual; whereas the most agonizing thing is when people are together, forced to be together. Everyone hates being in the army, sleeping in a dormitory or working in a team. In this kind of situation people can no longer communicate, because fellow-workers are not the same as friends. Quite the opposite, in fact: under such circumstances you feel constrained, alienated. And alienation in the Stalinist countries is a thousand times more terrible than bourgeois alienation.

C.B.   Solitude, then, is not dramatic.

E.I.   What is dramatic is the loneliness of the crowd, enforced proximity, outwardly being with other people all the time. Being crammed together like sardines.

C.B. Isn't this kind of enforced proximity the opposite of real emotional or intellectual communication?

E.I. Yes. Eugenio D'Ors said that for him humanity was a kind of great assembly in which Kant replied to Plato, while Marx held a dialogue with Hegel and Dante reproached Virgil for something or other, and so on. This true society, this ideal meeting of friends is impossible without solitude or withdrawal.

C.B. But even setting aside its implications as a parable, the dialogue that Eugenio D'Ors imagined is essentially a cultural or philosophical one. Does this comparison have any practical application outside the sphere of culture?

E.I. Life has to be thoroughly impregnated with solitude in order to be liveable. Everyone needs a personal space to live in. All these things are quite obvious; I'm only saying them to make it quite clear that I have never thought solitude undesirable. Quite the contrary—it is indispensible; and indeed my characters are simply people who don't know how to be alone. They have no conception of contemplation, of withdrawal. And this is a lack, an emptiness. That's why in certain of my plays, the characters are always with one another and always chattering. They are noisy because they have forgotten the meaning and value of solitude. And this is why they are alone—alone in a quite different way. There is noise in *A Stroll in the Air* too, people talking, saying any old thing because they are cut off, separated from themselves and therefore from other people. In *The Killer*, also, there are scenes where the characters are together, looking at one another and talking to one another in a completely depersonalized way. Look at crowds, they're depersonalized, people don't have 'faces' in a crowd. People become faceless when they form groups that are too large; or if they have a face, it's a collective face, and monstrous. It is the face of anger, of destruction, the face of hell. Everyone has the same face in a crowd, whether it is uniform or formless.

C.B. So, basically then, you are elaborating upon Kierkegaard's statement that, 'The worst dumbness is not to be silent, but to talk'.

There is one kind of solitude in your work that interests me particularly—that of Bérenger at the end of *Rhinoceros*, where he is the only man left among the monsters, the only lucid consciousness among a crowd of alienated beings. What does this solitude mean for you?

E.I. Bérenger finds himself alone in a dehumanized world where everyone has wanted to be like everyone else. It's because they've wanted to become like other people that they've been dehumanized—or rather depersonalized, it's basically the same thing. Though perhaps there is another side to it. These people have given up their humanity, that is to say, they've renounced their own lives, their own personalities; it's possible that they may find a certain joy, a certain animal happiness in this abdication.

It's very odd. This play about solitude and individualism has been performed everywhere. It's been more successful than any other of my plays. So then people said: 'It is the masses who enjoy this play. Isn't that a ludicrous contradiction?' To which I reply: 'No.' I think that if this play has been well received all over the world, it's because nowadays all countries, in the West as well as the East, are more or less collectivized. Almost unconsciously I put my finger on a terrible problem: that of depersonalization. Now in all modern societies collectivized individuals long for solitude, for a personal life. According to Jean-Louis Barrault, what the play aroused in audiences all over the world was the Bérenger who lies within each of us. A man with a soul is not like every other man.

C.B.   In a way Bérenger is the embodiment of contemporary man, of solitary man, in so far as he. . . .

E.I.   . . . is a man who tries to take his solitude upon himself, who tries not to abdicate, who resists 'rhinoceritis'. Every soul is unique; no one *is* other people, everyone has to be *with* other people.

C.B.   So isn't the solitary man in fact the person who is most concerned for the dignity of other people?

E.I.   Yes, I think so. Mindful of his own dignity, he is naturally mindful of others', because he wishes to safeguard what is in fact the essence of man's value, his uniqueness; *no one is replaceable*. It is in this way, in this solitude, that he finds friendship and a friendly society, rather than the flock or herd.

C.B.   With Bérenger's solitude then, you are posing a problem that is more than sociological; you are dealing with the very problem of the human condition.

E.I.   I'm not sure. Perhaps. That's all there is. Anyway, what I mean is . . . I think one should re-read Camus . . . and Emmanuel Mounier, starting with his *Manifeste du Personnalisme*.

Claude Bonnefoy. About ten years ago, critics chose the phrase 'theatre of the absurd' to designate the new theatre. Martin Esslin chose this as the title for his collection of essays on writers as different as Beckett, Adamov, Tardieu, Genet, Albee, Günter Grass and yourself. Do you feel you have anything in common with all these writers, or do you feel quite different from them?

Eugène Ionesco. I hope we are all different from one another. I also believe we're alike, and that among so-called 'absurd' writers one could also include the really great dramatists: Shakespeare, Sophocles and Aeschylus, Chekhov, Pirandello and O'Neill, all the writers who've ever existed, great and small. The 'absurd' is a very vague notion. Maybe it's the failure to understand something, some universal laws. It is born of the conflict between my will and a universal will; it is also born of the conflict within me between me and myself, between my different wills, my contradictory impulses: I want simultaneously to live and to die, or rather, I have within me a movement both towards death and towards life. *Eros* and *thanatos*, love and hatred, love and destruction, it's a sufficiently violent antithesis, isn't it, to give me a feeling of 'absurdity'. How can you construct any sort of logic on this basis, even a 'dialectical' logic?

C.B. When we were talking about non-communication, you said: 'Non-communication was a fashionable word, like absurd'. But doesn't a fashionable word in some way correspond to the preoccupations of an age, and don't writers—consciously or otherwise—reflect these preoccupations?

E.I. In a sense, when a thing or an idea, is fashionable, it's often mere repetition—a cliché emptied of its content, its truth, its discovery. On the other hand, obviously every work is rooted in time. And if it doesn't express the times it's written in, the anguish of its times, the problems or some part of the problems of its times, it's no good. It's no good because it has no substance or historical reality, in other words no living reality. Of course, this is all fairly obvious. Yet every worthwhile work is an original work that offers something which was not known before. The whole history of literature is the history of its expression. At the same time if the characters described in a work are too closely linked to their era, they become the expressions of an inadequate, restricted humanity. Which is why all worthwhile literary works stand at the crossroads between time and eternity, at the ideal point of universality.

Take the themes of Beckett's or Adamov's plays which express the absurd condition of man: man is going to die; man has limits; man doesn't accept his destiny and yet he does have a destiny; what is the meaning of this destiny? What is the meaning of the fact that man can give no meaning to his destiny? etc. . . . these are not just contemporary themes or problems. They've become more acute, more striking because of certain contemporary situations and events. These themes can be found in periods known as periods of crisis, though all periods are more of less ones of crisis, since everything is a crisis. So that these themes recur throughout the whole history of art. They can be found throughout the history of the theatre. With the Greeks, for instance, wherever there is fate, a conflict between man and his fate, there's an intuitive sense of the absurd, evidence of the absurd. Also, as I think I've said several times before, Beckett reminds me of Job. So there is a kind of permanence. For two thousand years, men have at certain moments experienced this truth of the absurd, if I may put it like that, and have asked themselves the essential questions. As for the contemporary theatre of the absurd, what distinguishes it from the *théâtre de boulevard* is that the latter does not pose the problem of the human condition or of its ultimate purpose, whereas Beckett's plays do nothing else.

C.B.   Do you think that Beckett, Adamov or you yourself

121

have been influenced by the philosophies of the absurd for which—in France—Sartre, and more particularly Camus, were the principal spokesmen after the war?

E.I. The notion of the absurd was very much in the air at the time. In other words, the post-war period enabled us to be more acutely aware of certain realities which were not simply realities of the period. We, and I as much as anyone, were certainly influenced by some of the things we read; though I find it hard to say which books in particular. We are always influenced by what we live through, by what we see, by what we read—and the authors we read have in their turn been influenced by the age in which they live, by what they have read and seen and lived through.

C.B. Isn't it curious that when they turned to writing plays, authors like Sartre and Camus who had discussed the absurd from a philosophical point of view, were happy to borrow from mythology or ancient history, Electra and Caligula—this would confirm what you were saying just now—and that at the same time they should have kept within the limits of a traditional theatrical aesthetic! However interesting their plays may be, they do in fact seem to be far closer in time to Sardou than to either Brecht or Beckett and Ionesco. On the other hand it seems to me that Beckett, Adamov and yourself started out less from philosophical reflections or a return to classical sources, than from first-hand experience and a desire to find a new theatrical expression that would enable you to render this experience in all its acuteness and also its immediacy. If Sartre and Camus thought out these themes, you expressed them in a far more vital and contemporary fashion.

E.I. I have the feeling that these writers—who are serious and important—were talking about absurdity and death, but that they never really lived these themes, that they did not feel them within themselves in an almost irrational, visceral way, that all this was not deeply inscribed in their language. With them it was still rhetoric, eloquence. With Adamov and Beckett it really is a very naked reality that is conveyed through the apparent dislocation of language. What once looked like the dislocation of language now seems very clear to us. The way of expressing a certain disaster is starting to congeal again and increasing the distance between us and the disaster. This disjointed language has reconstituted itself in another way; or rather, the dislocation, having as it were congealed, now looks to us like a new coherence ... perhaps I should say, like a new crust, an armour. This is why the great themes, the essential themes, have always to be reworked, relived, re-expressed.

C.B.   Doesn't the absurdity of your theatre derive on the one hand from that amazement at the world which you discussed in our earlier conversations, and on the other from a desire to communicate raw reality, everyday human behaviour, without trying to explain or to justify this reality and this behaviour?

E.I.   Rather than 'absurd' I prefer the expression 'unusual' or feeling of the unusual. There are times when the world seems emptied of all expression, all content. There are times when we look at it as though we'd just that moment been born, and then it looks astonishing and inexplicable. Of course, we have plenty of explanations to hand! We've been given plenty of them and we have a variety of systems of thought at our disposal. Only these systems fade the moment we have this primordial feeling, this fundamental intuition, that we are here, that something exists and that this something demands to be explained. At this point, all systems of thought, all explanations appear inadequate; the more so because these systems explain what is happening from a basis of something that is unformulated: this monolithic, inexplicable presence of the world and of existence, which ideologies, moralities and sociologies avoid, turning their backs on it or else standing gaping on the doorstep.

C.B. This notion of the *déjà là*, of being already there, makes one think of all those exegeses in German philosophy about the term 'Dasein' from Hegel to Heidegger. Were you influenced at all by this philosophy?

E.I. Each time you read a philosopher, either you retain him or you don't. You retain what he says if you've already lived through similar experiences. Philosophy is poetry as well—and I think Heidegger is not unfamiliar with this view of philosophy. I should say that we have all had feelings of this sort, of wonder at what's already there, of existence. Just as, before I'd read Pascal, I'd already felt at the age of ten or twelve the terror of 'infinite spaces': everyone has had this awakening. And at about seventeen or eighteen I had that experience of illumination, of light, that I talked to you about at the beginning of our conversations. The philosophers I've managed to blunder my way through did perhaps amplify and clarify what was still for me just an elementary intuition.

C.B. Since you think the theatre should not be ideological, at least not directly, do you think it should also not be philosophical?

E.I. The theatre should not be philosophical, but since all poetry is philosophy, inevitably it's philosophical in an indirect way. Isn't it philosophical to become aware that one is facing the world and to ask oneself the question 'what is it?'

C.B. That's the first question of philosophy.

E.I. And it's never solved. . . . In a certain sense, everything is philosophy, or rather comes from it. The theatre too

124

derives from this questioning. In fact it has to stem from it, or risk being inadequate and insignificant. Only, once again, let's say philosophy and not philosophical doctrine, philosophy and not ideology. Art is philosophical in so far as philosophy means exploration, posing problems, questioning, adopting an attitude. What I call ideology is a closed system, giving 'clichéized' explanations.

C.B. Do your plays express your attitude to the world?

E.I. That's a very difficult question. I think that in the things I've written there are some works which try to express this basic attitude that is at the root of everything, this first questioning of the world. There are others which express less important preoccupations, political or social ones, and these deal with behaviour, psychology, love. In other plays, I simply amuse myself without any deeper intention. I think those which most express the fundamental primordial astonishment are my comic plays. It may seem odd; but that's how it seems to me. In *The Chairs*, there's the whirlwind of chairs that expresses the evanescence, the loneliness of a world which is there, which isn't there, which will cease to be. You can find the same thing in other plays like *The Killer*, although even there it's already slightly different. In *The Killer*, in the first act, the main character (this is Bérenger's début) is amazed at his existence, at being in the world; and he finds this extraordinary and marvellous. So that there, at that point, he's acting out the fundamental attitude. But later, this wondrous world falls apart, disintegrates. There's the problem of hatred, the problem of death, etc. . . . Already these important problems—important not because of the way I've treated them but important in themselves—are less important than the primordial, fundamental attitude. This attitude is almost indescribable; and if we were simply to stop at it, then obviously everyday existence, history, all kinds of problems would simply not exist. We don't always live on the same level of consciousness.

C.B. Isn't this primordial attitude equally conducive—and this is what makes it possible to write both 'light' and 'dark' plays—to wonderment, uneasiness and anguish?

E.I. This astonishment at being sometimes leads to unease and anguish, sometimes to wonderment. This wonderment at being isn't a permanent state, obviously, since I am here, since we are living, since I am writing plays instead of living a solitary life of contemplation or questioning without writing at all. It seems to me that literature is produced, primarily, to express this straying from the narrow path, this fall, this abandoning in spite of ourselves of the primordial state which is very close to the paradisiacal state.

C.B. Isn't literature also a means of regaining that primordial state, that moment of ecstasy which could neither be sustained nor forgotten?

E.I. I don't think so. It's precisely here—it seems to me—that literature has in a sense become bankrupt: all literature seems to me to be created first and foremost to express personal life, historical life, life in a temporal context, or else to express the fall.

C.B. But doesn't expressing the fall imply a nostalgia for the summit, the first beginnings?

E.I. Clearly, it's a summit that becomes increasingly distant.

C.B. Isn't this quest or longing for the summit, for the beginning, one of the ways in which the absurd expresses itself? Isn't it absurd in itself because we know it's a summit on which we shall never be able to remain?

E.I.   What you say contains one valid connotation of the absurd. But what is absurd, or rather what is unusual, is first and foremost what exists, reality. I realize I use the word *absurd* to express what are often very different concepts. There are several sorts of 'absurd' things or facts. Sometimes, I use the word to describe what I don't understand—and this can either be because I'm not capable of understanding it or because the thing itself is incomprehensible, impenetrable, closed, like this thick monolithic hunk of reality, this wall which I see as a sort of massive, solidified void, a block of mystery; I use the word 'absurd' to describe my position in relation to this mystery; my state, which is to find myself faced with a wall which is as high as the sky and which extends as far as the infinite frontiers, which is to say the non-frontiers of the universe, and which I cannot prevent myself from doggedly trying to climb over or break through, even while knowing at the same time that this is impossibility itself; absurd, therefore, this situation of being here that I cannot recognize as being my situation; but which is mine, all the same. Another example of what I call absurd is man wandering without purpose—forgetful of his purpose, cut off from his essential, transcendental roots (aimless wandering is Kafka's kind of absurdity).

All this is the experience of metaphysical absurdity, of the absolute enigma; but there's also a kind of absurdity that is unreason, contradiction, the expression of my being out of tune with the world, of my being profoundly out of tune with myself, of the world being out of tune with itself. The absurd is also quite simply illogicality, unreason; so that history is not strictly speaking absurd, in the sense we've just established—it's nonsensical. It's difficult to see any of this very clearly, it would take a lot of sorting out.

C.B.   But in these conditions, wouldn't you say that history, which is a central concern of many of our contemporaries, including many dramatists, is also absurd?

E.I. I would say that history is nonsensical or that the explanations given of it are unreasonable, whereas an explanation ought ideally to be possible. So what strikes me as absurd, utterly extraordinary, is existence in itself! An essential insufficiency, a limit of our understanding: I might say more accurately that I don't understand it.

As for history—well, what is history? It's men who perform actions, good actions or more usually bad ones, who invent an absurd world for themselves because they put themselves in positions of contradiction with themselves. The moment there's a gap between ideology and reality, there's absurdity. It's not the same absurdity, it's a feeling of practical, moral absurdity, not of metaphysical absurdity. But it is almost as though man wanted this absurdity. Maybe it's man himself who creates the absurdity of history because we no longer know what laws history obeys. It has often been said that history obeyed certain laws. The direction of history, the course of history—what exactly does it mean? One can find a reason for any action. In which case, the absurd—the historical absurd—simply dissolves. But isn't the reason which impels us to act itself absurd? Can one say that reason isn't a reason? Perhaps it's 'absurd' to look for a reason for everything. In short, perhaps I don't believe that history is reasonable, nor that it is always unreasonable. Men are sometimes reasonable, but they also allow themselves to be led on by all sorts of unreasonableness, which is why history is both reasonable and unreasonable. The reasonable is itself unreasonable in relation to another Reason. In fact, language does nothing but contradict at every moment an extremely simple and visible reality, as if everyone were refusing to see this reality.

As a result, countries which oppress say they are liberators, tyranny takes the name of freedom, vengeance the name of justice; and men speak of love and friendship where there is only indifference and rancour.

C.B. So what we need is for what is said to tally with what actually is.

E.I. What we need is a constant work of clarification and definition, the abolition of the political 'absurd' ... which is different from the fundamental absurd.

C.B. But who could carry out this work?

E.I. I could if I were helped. ... No, I'm joking. But I do believe that if there were a hundred people in the world working with the statue of objectivity before their eyes, the world could be saved. But instead of this our thoughts are always confused, we are carried away by our emotions.

C.B. Is absolute objectivity possible? Could the artist or the writer go beyond his subjectivity, his dreams, his emotions, to contribute to the setting up or the defence of this objectivity?

E.I. Objectivity is good faith. Subjectivities can link up. To know truth, in its subjectivity and beyond its subjectivity, is what Socrates and Plato taught us; then Freud, Jung and others. We can see beyond our subjectivity, there are methods for achieving this; we can do it, for instance, by putting ourselves in other people's places: in this way we escape from ourselves. (Where do passions come from? And why? This can be analysed.) Passions can be clarified, purged or modified.

Claude Bonnefoy. We have already talked about the connections between the comic and the tragic in your work. The comic appears at several levels in your plays. Situational comedy, mechanical comedy, playing on words or rather playing with words—these alternate or overlap as the scenes allow. What is particularly noticeable, and what helps to bring out the absurdity or the unexpectedness of the world, is your 'black' humour. What does humour mean for you.

Eugène Ionesco. People have said that my theatre was humorous, that I had a sense of humour. What is humour? Laughing at misfortune, and at one's own misfortune perhaps.

C.B. Isn't this humour something very different from the type of comedy that exists in the *théâtre de boulevard*?

E.I. There's a type of comedy you get when the characters find themselves in embarrassing or incongruous situations. We feel quite clearly that all situations are not comic. It is humour that puts across the humorist's feeling that everything is unreasonable, ludicrous, that we're all from the moment we're born in an unexplained and inexplicable situation.

C.B. Isn't it also a way of not being taken in, of keeping one's distance from the absurd or the tragic?

E.I. Exactly. It's also a way of denouncing absurdity, of going beyond drama. Humour presupposes a lucid consciousness. It presupposes a split-level consciousness, a lucid awareness of the vanity of our own passions. We then continue to experience these passions while knowing that they are absurd or stupid, even if we can't put up much of a struggle against them. In other words, humour is becoming aware of absurdity while continuing to live in absurdity.

C.B. Could you give me an example of such a situation?

E.I. All situations are humorous and all situations are tragic.
. . . You want an example. There is no point in loathing
someone. But I loathe him just the same. But I know that
it's pointless. It's ridiculous to be in love because no one
is adorable, and at the same time you go on being in love,
even though you realize that it's ridiculous. Humour
enables you to experience a whole range of passions
while realizing that they are absolutely meaningless.

C.B. Are you sure that being in love is absolutely meaningless?

E.I. It's being caught in a trap, a psychological or biological
or physiological trap or all three at once. It's being taken
in (I'm talking now from the humorist's point of view!).
To feel anything at all, to suffer from anything at all, is
to be taken in. Humour consists of realizing this while
continuing to feel love or pain. Indeed, complete demystification would be death. But through humour,
there is a continuous distancing effect.

C.B. We are at once both actors and spectators. In one way,
isn't this the ideal theatrical situation?

E.I. The theatre should be this and nothing more. The
theatre is man offering himself as a spectacle for his own
entertainment.

C.B. This implies that the spectator recognizes himself in the
author.

E.I. If he doesn't, it's because one of them, either the writer or
the spectator, is lacking in intelligence.

C.B. Very often it's in language that humour is most obviously
present in your plays. It begins with plays on words or

with unusual verbal juxtapositions. Exactly how much importance do you attach to these linguistic games?

E.I. None. Which is why I use them. If they were important, I wouldn't. Do I enjoy them? Well, of course I do. Playing with words, doing anything at all with words is a liberation. Give words a complete freedom, make them say anything at all, without any purpose in mind, and something will always emerge. There will always be words linked together which, just because they're linked, will have some meaning. But when people seize on this meaning and say: 'That's what the man who wrote these sentences meant to say', when he didn't mean to say anything at all, it's the greatest disappointment an author can experience.

C.B. When this happens, do you feel that people don't understand what you were trying to do?

E.I. When I'm writing, sometimes I want to say things that mean a lot to me because, like everyone else, I have moments when I'm imprisoned by my passions, imprisoned by a certain conformism, by certain ideas; and sometimes I don't want to say anything at all. These are the happiest and apparently the least significant moments; but precisely because they are the least significant, they are perhaps the most significant.

C.B. When a critic interprets these passages, do you feel that he's fallen into the trap of your words or do you feel that he's throwing an interesting light on them that you had not foreseen?

E.I. Sometimes one, sometimes the other. Sometimes he hasn't understood, sometimes he gives these series of words, this verbal irruption, a meaning that I recognize.

C.B. Your plays often include long strings of words that would be perfectly logical except for the sudden introduction of one or two words which bear no relation to the others and which therefore disrupt their meaning. And it is these alien words that highlight the verbal mechanism of enumeration and give the whole thing a humorous note. For instance in *The Chairs* when Semiramis lists the guests who are going to come—wardens, bishops, chemists, etc.—she suddenly includes penholders and chromosomes in the list. Doesn't she, by doing this, indicate that all the characters she's mentioned were imaginary, and that enumerating them was gratuitous and absurd?

E.I. Obviously, there's an association of sounds. It's a game. The words emerge and follow one another by free association. There is a certain gratuitousness in it. But what does this gratuitousness mean, and is it really as gratuitous as all that? It does mean something, all the same.

C.B. Aren't these associations similar to the free associations used in psychoanalysis and don't they sometimes reveal certain images or certain themes? Let's take, for instance, this passage from *Jacques or Obedience* where Roberta expresses herself in an apparently incoherent manner:[1] 'I'm all moist . . . I've a necklace of ooze, my breasts are melting, my pelvis is soft, I've water in my crevices. I'm getting bogged in. My real name is Blodwen. In my womb there are ponds and swamps . . . I've a house of clay . . . where I always feel cool . . . where there's foamy loam . . . and fatty flies, beetles, woodlice and toads. Beneath dripping blankets we make love. . . . Swelling with bliss! My arms enfold you like snakes; and my soft thighs . . . you plunge deep and dissolve . . . in the rain of my streaming hair. My mouth is streaming, streaming, my shoulders bare, my hair is streaming, everything

[1] NOTE: as translated by Donald Watson in Eugène Ionesco: *Plays*, Vol. I (London: Calder).

flows and streams, the sky's a stream, the stars strow and fleam. . . .'

E.I.   Yes, obviously this isn't the same type of association we were discussing before. In the enumeration in *The Chairs*, the words 'pope, popinjays, paper' had no meaning for me. They are sounds, more or less stripped of sense. Here, I have the feeling that the words and images are connected. When Roberta says 'My mouth is streaming, steaming my legs, my shoulders bare, etc.', I make her say 'streaming' because it seems to me to be stronger than 'dripping'. When she says: 'I'm bogged in. My real name is Blodwen', it's because I myself was foundering or because I felt that the character was foundering and I wanted to give her a burst of freedom.

C.B.   Does this mean that by stating a situation one can free oneself from the anguish it produces?

E.I.   For a second Roberta escapes from the anguish and the foundering. It's like someone who is drowning and who then, suddenly, has a burst of energy, or rather it's like someone who sees himself sinking.

C.B.   Yes. But when after 'I'm bogged in' she says 'my real name is Blodwen'; doesn't the fact that she calls herself by a name which, incidentally, is not her own, have some meaning? Isn't it an attempt to call herself by a different name, to become someone different who will either escape from this foundering or else experience it in her place? I am thinking of those ancient magical systems in which names had the power of talismans, in which the name was one with the person named, an affirmation of existence.

E.I.   It's true, here she is affirming her independence of this foundering. You're making what I wrote here clearer to me. However, I knew what I wanted to say in this passage. They're dream images, certainly, but selected ones, all intended to express the material nature, the non-spirituality of sexuality: man's foundering in eroticism.

C.B. Do you regard eroticism as something very material?

E.I. Not always. But in the present case, it's pure biology. It's a sort of abdication of consciousness. Here, the characters escape from psychology and logic, they escape from the everyday mentality. And from dreams, too. Jacques escapes from society and loses his soul to sink into a reality that is purely biological. He is dominated by the material world.

C.B. To return to the problem of language. In *Jacques or Obedience*, language is utilized in other ways. I'm thinking for instance of the song Roberta II sings, which contains the simultaneous affirmation of contradictory facts or ideas:[1]

> *There's no one else like me on earth.*
> *I'm full of light and gloom and mirth.*
> *I'm neither frivolous nor gloomy.*
> *I can make a room look roomy.*
> *Other things also I can do.*
> *Bigger, better, badder too.*
> *I'm exactly right for you.*
> *I am honest and deceitful*
> *With me your life will be repleteful.*
> *On the piano I can play*
> *Scales until I get my way.*
> *My education's sound as sound,*
> *I've been uniformed and gowned.*

Isn't this a rejection of dialectic since all the terms are given simultaneously; and isn't it an attempt at describing a character in all its most contradictory aspects, with each aspect being considered as true as the next?

[1] NOTE: Ibid.

E.I. Let's say it's meant to be about a perfect woman. A model woman who has everything a man could ask for. She is also a divinity in whom all contradictory attributes come together.

C.B. And the three-nosed mask therefore expresses these contradictory attributes. It's their outward and visible manifestation.

E.I. This is a woman who has not just three faces but an infinity of faces, since she is all women.

C.B. At the end of *Jacques or Obedience*, Roberta wants to name everything by the same one word: puss.
'The cats are called puss; food, puss; insects, puss; chairs, puss; number two, puss; three, puss; number one, puss; all the adverbs, puss; all the prepositions, puss. It makes talking so easy.'[1]
Can we not see in this a desire for a sort of universal language?

E.I. It's rather an absence of language, non-differentiation; everything is on the same level, it's the abdication of lucidity, and liberty, when faced with the organic world.

C.B. Doesn't every writer, every poet, feel the temptation of silence?

E.I. There's silence and silence. In *Jacques* it's a question of what I might call an inferior silence. There is another silence, a luminous silence. There is in *Jacques*, I think, one of those two states that I experience alternately, of heaviness and weightlessness, light and darkness. On the other side of the silence of light there lies the silence of mud.

C.B. If calling everything 'puss' is an absence of language,
[1] NOTE: Ibid.

doesn't *The Bald Prima Donna* contain a criticism of ready-made, automatized language, which is in fact a sort of sub-language? But by its insistence on banalities, by its statement of the obvious, Mrs. Smith's language becomes equally unexpected. And yet it's familiar because since the play, whenever one catches oneself uttering several consecutive clichés in a conversation, it sounds like mock-Ionesco. What led you to compose this language?

E.I.   I started with clichés, reflex phrases, ready-made truths. There comes a point when these truths go berserk. It comes from the fact that the characters are puppets, members of the universal petty-bourgeoisie. They live on slogans. Basically, all I had to do was to listen to the people around me talking. They talked like students of the Assimil method.[1] They are themselves automatons: they have a sub-language.

C.B.   At the present time, linguists are talking about a gulf between spoken language, that of the average contemporary Frenchman, and written language, which has been codified by the grammarians and Littré and which is still remarkably close to the language of the eighteenth century. What's striking in Beckett's work and in your own, and also in novelists like Céline or Queneau (as you see the range is wide), is that while successfully utilizing the spoken language, you somehow all manage to re-invent it, to give it an aesthetic value it did not previously have and which is comparable to that of classical French. Were you yourself aware of undertaking anything of this kind?

E.I.   What I wanted above all was to say certain things, even by not saying them, and I was more concerned about this than about the way I said them: the language came with them, it just tacked itself on.

[1] NOTE: The English equivalent would be 'on a Linguaphone record'.

137

Claude Bonnefoy. *Improvisation, or The Shepherd's Chameleon* has as its subject the dialogue between author and critics, the confrontation of different conceptions of the theatre; yet at the same time it follows the structure characteristic of all your works, a movement from the banal and the real through to the fantastic or the unusual. Is the theatre a good subject for the theatre?

Eugène Ionesco. Everything can be a good subject for the theatre, even the theatre. It depends on what you do with it. If you treat a theme according to the rules of the novel, it is a novel. Treat it according to the laws of the theatre, it's a play. *Improvisation* is a play in which I try to imitate Molière, and it's also a criticism of various critics. I reproach the critics for their dogmatism, their failure to understand art, their refusal to understand the theatre. The critics I present in the play are militant critics.

C.B. There is also the critic who likes nothing but *théâtre de boulevard*.

E.I. Well, I could hardly leave him out. The two main characters, Bartholomeus I and Bartholomeus II, are dogmatic critics. The theatre doesn't exist for them; doesn't interest them. It can interest them only in so far as it's an instrument of propaganda. For what political sect? Impossible to say, because these critics, though they call themselves Marxists, are in fact petit bourgeois with political ambitions, a desire for power. In other words, as far as they're concerned, the theatre ought to be the instrument of their particular politics, and authors ought to observe the regulations they lay down. Which would be very difficult: the artistic process, which consists of creation and exploration, cannot be confined to illustrating a thesis.

C.B. What is interesting in *The Shepherd's Chameleon* is that

138

you have created something that is both a thesis play—
in so far as you are defending the freedom of creation
against the demands of contradictory theories—and a
drama—because it shows the author grappling with
theoreticians of the theatre. And when theatre becomes
drama, it's no longer a lesson, or at least, it's more than a
single lesson.

E.I.   It's a lesson that is, as it were, the consequence of a drama.
The author in the play is assailed by the different critics
who are trying to impose on him a particular way of
writing, a mode of thinking: this was in the days of
Brechtian tyranny, or of a tyranny that the Parisian
Brechtians—revolutionaries without an army and one or
two revolutions behind the times—were trying to impose. It could have been the basis for an interesting discussion, but 'Brechtianism' admitted of neither discussion
nor co-existence; it was therefore a threat to one's intelligence. It was this threat that I was rebelling against. The
play was to some extent a montage of texts taken from
magazines like *Théâtre Populaire*, *Bref* and, for a few
sentences, from *Le Figaro*. Dr. Bartholomeus' theories
about costumology can be found in the works of Roland
Barthes. One day Barthes discovered that the theatre
could be a vehicle of propaganda, of instruction. So then
he started going to the theatre, and he produced a theory
of costumology that was both pedantic, academic and,
at the same time, simplistic and rudimentary, because he
was discovering things that had been discovered long
ago, that any amateur who's produced so much as half a
play already knows. For instance: there must be no
contradiction, but perfect balance, between the scenery
and the actual performance; the costumes must not be
more elegant, colourful or eye-catching than the rest of
the play, they must be an integral part of that totality
which any production is, etc.

C.B.   On this point I don't agree with you. Granted that these

139

are well-known truths, they're also truths that are all too often forgotten. Barthes was thinking of the *théâtre de boulevard* or of those musicals where the sets and costumes are more important than the text and, worse still, where the sets and costumes exist to delight the eye but are completely unrelated to the actors' performances.

E.I.   Yes. Sometimes in the *théâtre de boulevard*, and even in other plays, the décor, the spectacular side, is more important than the play. But that's the whole point of this kind of show. The text here is only a pretext for an amusing or lavish entertainment. It may be successful or otherwise, but people have the right to produce such things without bringing the thunderbolts of the learned doctors down upon their heads. They also have the right to produce 'entertainment for entertainment's sake'. In other plays, the balance is respected, quite naturally.

C.B.   Yes, but there is a difference between certain shows in which every person plays his part, where the designer, actor and author can be applauded separately, and others like *A Stroll in the Air* or *Rhinoceros*, where the sets, if they're to be any good, must express certain symbols and be an integral part of the production as a whole.

E.I.   Most of the time, the sets are pretty well integrated. I've seen productions of Shakespeare, of Racine, Molière, Kleist, Büchner or Strindberg, where there was almost always a complete integration. What irritated Barthes and the dogmatic critics was that people would applaud the sets. But people have the right to applaud the sets just as they occasionally applaud a particular line that an actor speaks, an exit or an entrance, etc.; this doesn't mean that the set is harmful to the unity of the play. In my opinion one could just as well go to a big couturier's and watch the mannequins file past. That, too, is a kind of theatrical production. It isn't set in the framework of a theatre, but it offers us women wearing lavish or elegant costumes. So there are some shows where sets, and costumes, have the main role. That they have no text, or little text, is neither here nor there. The danger would be to produce no other shows but these. But it's not a trend I can see taking over in our theatres. In any case, it's the 'didactic' entertainment—not the type of play that our learned theoreticians call 'bourgeois'—which unbalances, disrupts and falsifies a theatrical work; the type of play where the production style is more important than the text and deforms it in the name of 'remodernizing' the work, in order to make it say things it never meant to say but which fit in with a particular ideology. The productions by Stanislavsky and his French and German followers, for instance, were real catastrophes. . . . They completely shattered and unbalanced the unity of the works in question, but one wasn't allowed to object to that . . . I don't think the 'theoreticians' even noticed it.

C.B.   What I find interesting about *Improvisation* is that you do in fact answer the critics. You say that the theatre should first and foremost be theatrical. What exactly does theatrical mean?

E.I.   That's a very awkward question. I wonder if anyone's managed to define the theatrical or theatricality? Particularly since we started producing 'anti-theatre' and believing it was theatrical just the same. The exponents of theatrology also talk about the theatrical, and theatricality.

C.B.   They start off by contrasting entertainment plays with educational ones.

E.I.   Neither entertainment nor education really exhausts the idea of the theatre. There can be lessons and entertainments which are theatrical, and others which are not. What is the theatre? That's the really difficult question.

C.B. Which you answer by creating plays, the way people prove movement by walking.

E.I. What is the theatre? Is it the exposition of a conflict? Perhaps. But the epic theatre is not particularly the presentation of a conflict and nowadays people want theatre to be epic. Is conflict what theatre's all about? A football match is a conflict too. Does that make it theatrical? It's a spectacle, like a bullfight where there is also the element of conflict. But it's equally possible to have a theatre without conflict. . . . Everything is possible in the theatre. We can be shown something happening on the stage, or just someone walking across it, stopping and looking. We may be shown lighting effects, pieces of scenery, a silhouette, animals . . . or we can be shown a bare stage. Whatever people say, it's all theatre. The theatre is whatever is shown on a stage. That's the simplest definition, but also the least unjust, the vaguest . . . and the hardest to contradict. To sum up, we all know more or less what theatre is, otherwise we wouldn't be able to talk about it: perhaps you could define it as moving architecture, a living, dynamic construction built of antagonisms. As for my own work, the theatre for me is a way of presenting something rather rare, rather strange, rather monstrous. It's something terrible which is gradually revealed with the progress not of the action (unless one puts the word in quotation marks) but of a series of more or less complex events or states. The theatre is a kind of succession of states and situations moving towards an increasing densification.

C.B. You used the word 'monstrous'. If the theatre is a succession of internal and external situations, what—if you'll allow the question—is it that is monstrous? Is it the theatre, life or yourself?

E.I. Life, myself, the character I put on to the stage, the event which is suddenly revealed. For me the theatre is all this as well. I have the feeling of being among extremely polite people, in a more or less comfortable world. Suddenly something breaks loose and rips, and man's monstrous nature is revealed, or else the décor takes on an inconceivable strangeness, and perhaps in this way men and décor reveal their true nature. Perhaps that's what theatre is: the revelation of something that was hidden. The theatre is the appearance of the unexpected; it's surprise. I won't use the word demystification, even though it seems appropriate, because demystification is itself a mystification, especially because nowadays it has so many familiar ideological or political associations. What should be demystified is demystification—its clichés. Demystifying with clichés . . . what a contradiction! But what I'm trying to say is that the theatre shouldn't be an illustration of something already postulated. On the contrary, it's an exploration. And it is because of this process, this exploration, that one arrives at the revelation of a truth which is most often unbearable, but which can also be luminous and comforting.

C.B. Isn't it a way of hunting down your own monsters?

E.I. Yes. If people have found my plays interesting, and I can't help feeling they have, it's because my monsters are not private ones, they're common to a lot of people, universal monsters perhaps, or at least the monsters of a particular universe. This is the area in which an author and his public seek one another and recognize one another. The most personal theatre is also the most social. There's been a lot of talk about a popular theatre, a social theatre; people have said that the writer must not be cut off from his fellows, that he must work for society. These are truisms. Every author does this instinctively. The theorists and scholars too often confuse society with administrators or authorities, and this leads them to hide truth beneath an ideology or a moral code of some kind: they confuse dynamic contradiction with ideologies

143

which lead to the petrifying régimes set up elsewhere, but 'set up' and therefore quite liable to be thrown off: here, they are defended and affirmed, with a retrogressiveness that's mistaken for progress. The French are at their most conservative when they think they're being revolutionary. They consider it quite normal that the threat of censorship or imprisonment should exist in so many countries, although they would find it completely unacceptable in France. An author is someone who discovers through his own individuality truths more universal than those imposed by ideologies or ruling castes of any sort.

C.B. You said before that neither instruction nor entertainment exhaust the concept of the theatrical. Do you mean by this that they fall short of it?

E.I. Well, in many cases they do fall short of it, which is why entertainment can be either theatrical or not theatrical. I can be amused in places other than the theatre. Similarly, if I can draw a lesson from a theatrical work, I can also draw the same lesson from many other things, from facts or experiences. For me, theatre has to be the revelation of hidden truths. Through the theatre, these must take on the appearance of living truths. But the didactic theatre reveals nothing, it contributes nothing new because it is dependent on existing ideologies, which it illustrates, and thereby repeats.

C.B. Rather than illustrating an ideology, isn't it the aim of the didactic theatre to throw light on a certain number of problems, to make the public aware of the existence of certain questions while leaving them free to make their own judgments?

E.I. The didactic theatre as it exists is rigidly controlled by the different propaganda centres, bureaux and clubs. It leaves no room for freedom of judgment. *Its very aim is to prevent* *freedom of judgment.* You're taught 'truths', you're enlightened, but it's a very special sort of enlightenment, one that is controlled, imposed. All the same, it's obvious that what's known as the didactic theatre can in certain cases be more than that, by which I mean that it can teach us things that the ideological theme didn't lead us to expect. The great dramatist is one who, even when he's trying to produce propaganda, goes beyond propaganda, beyond his initial intention. The creation of a theatrical work is a walk in the forest, an exploration, a conquest, the conquest of unknown realities, unknown sometimes to the author himself when he begins his work.

C.B. Isn't every great theatrical work the reflection of an age or, if not precisely situated in history, of the consciousness of its contemporaries?

E.I. Of course. It is both the expression of an age—but if it is only the reflection of an age, then it dies with that age, with the prevailing fashion—and the expression of a certain universality. It is also—in a far deeper, far more complete, more indirect, more deliberate and more spontaneous way—an expression of its author's uniqueness. When the author is alone, he expresses the world more fully than he could if the ruling powers were ordering him to represent a certain collective vision. Authorities, castes and parties necessarily constitute a closed society. Then again, I think that what interests the collectivity as a whole interests each of us, individually, very little. I think that each individual is more important, more real, more interesting than the group—above all, more universal. The individual is universal, the group has only a certain limited generality!

C.B. It seems to me that in your world you often tackle the problem of the meaning of the theatre, and also the problem of the mechanics of theatrical creation. Setting aside *Improvisation*, which is explicitly about the theatre, it seems to me significant that Nicolas in *Victims of Duty* should ask the policeman what he thinks about the theatre and even about the regeneration of the theatre; that there should be a playwright in *Amédée*; that in *Hunger and Thirst*, as in *Victims of Duty*, you should use the device—through some characters giving a performance to others—of the play within a play, a device that goes back to Rotrou's *Saint-Genest*. Doesn't this discussion of the theatre within the theatre reflect a permanent uneasiness, a constantly renewed search for the meaning of the theatre and the role of the dramatist?

E.I. Even when one is attempting to express certain inner truths, certain states, or more generally certain human truths, one is simultaneously thinking about the means of communicating them. This double process operates every time—hence the play within a play and the characters functioning on two levels, living out their dramas and thinking them at the same time.

C.B. So that you think a play is both its own mirror and the mirror of the author writing it?

E.I. It's obviously this in *Improvisation*, in *Victims of Duty* and in *Amédée*. In the other plays, it's less evident. In *The Bald Prima Donna*, as I've already said, I was trying to do several things at once; one of them was to demonstrate how bad a certain type of theatre is, and to do this by taking the theatrical mechanism apart.

C.B. Isn't Amédée's creative impotence, which expresses the drama of creation, the underlying theme of the play?

E.I. Partly, yes. His impotence is the result of his wondering whether literature has any validity at all, whether writing can bring him salvation. Ever since I started writing I've been asking myself whether it was worth it, or even if it was worth doing anything at all.

146

C.B. What is striking in *Amédée* is that you are showing us an author who is trying unsuccessfully to create an imaginary, fantastic world, and who, suddenly, in his own life finds himself face to face with the fantastic, i.e. with what he himself was trying to invoke by his writing. Doesn't this mean that the source of the fantastic lies in experience rather than in conscious and deliberate writing?

E.I. Maybe. All writing is conscious. Certainly when one writes one summons up fantasies, obsessions, things one doesn't oneself always understand clearly at the start. Through writing, these things acquire a meaning because they are grasped by consciousness and become known. It's a characteristic of art that it can make the unconscious conscious. In other words, it can translate the language of the depth of consciousness into everyday language. I don't know if I've managed to achieve this. But as I was saying before, creation is exploration. The author or main character is faced with the problem of knowing whether or not he ought to write. If someone doesn't or cannot write, it's because he doesn't believe in the usefulness of literature. Writing and not writing are both answers to the question.

C.B. What do you see as Amédée's answer, in his struggles with the written word?

E.I. It's the presence of those fantastic images that he draws out of himself, that he brings up to the level of his consciousness.

C.B. In fact, it's you who are bringing these images to the level of consciousness, since Amédée is incapable of completing his work and since it's his drama that you're putting on the stage.

E.I. Amédée's literature consists, basically, of his fantasies or his problems, his obsessions. And who wrote the play, who prompted whom? Him? Or me?

C.B. Presumably it was you, because the play isn't signed Amédée and isn't called *Ionesco or How to Get Rid of It*.

E.I. Of course, it's 'me'. It's not God. But it's another me who's revealing himself and talking.

C.B. I'd like to go back to the play within a play. In your last play *Hunger and Thirst*, two clowns, Tripp and Brechtoll, are giving a performance for Jean and the monks from the monastery, a performance which, in one way, is a parody of the didactic theatre. At the same time, this performance within a performance offers us, I think, a double mirror effect, with the monastery, the barracks and the prisons representing our society, and Tripp's and Brechtoll's play being the reflection of this society, highlighting its complexity and contradictions. Am I right?

E.I. Yes, to some extent. There is also the fact that all the beliefs for which we fight are of equal worth and that anyone who's placed in a different situation will believe the reverse of what he previously believed. It's a sort of levelling out of values, or of nihilism.

C.B. When you were attracted by this double mirror effect of the play within a play, were you thinking of Rotrou or Pirandello?

E.I. No, honestly, I wasn't. But I've certainly been influenced by everything I've seen or read, ever since I started seeing, reading or indeed living.

C.B. If you like showing the theatre within the theatre, isn't this because a dramatic performance sometimes gives the impression of being more fascinating than reality itself?

E.I. To say that reality becomes more real in the theatre is both true and false. It becomes more real in so far as we become aware of it through the theatre. If the theatre or any other system of expression helps us to become aware of reality, it's because imaginary reality is more valid, more full of potential than everyday reality. We live inside everyday reality without being aware of it, whereas an exploratory technique like literature or the theatre, for example, makes us understand it, brings us face to face with it. Through the theatre, through art, we are no longer submerged in this reality, we see it. But I must say that for some time now, literature has seemed to me to fall considerably short of the violence and intensity of real events; it can no longer grasp them, register them or illuminate them.

Today and Tomorrow

Claude Bonnefoy. You've said that for some time now literature has seemed to you to fall considerably short of the violence of real events. Could you be a little more specific about this?

Eugène Ionesco. Right now there's a rather bad type of literature being produced, the literature of the *nouveau roman*. In my opinion, it's a kind of psychosis, a sort of schizophrenia. The writers who go in for this type of literature place all kinds of obstacles between themselves and the world. They display an increasing disaffection for the world, whereas art and literature can only consist of responding to things, and knowing them through one's heart. But on the other hand, their works can't be considered philosophical because they don't go into things deeply enough.

What troubles me most is that they are turning their backs on the living truth. Two or three years ago, I read an article by Butor in *Le Figaro Littéraire*. This article had been written in Berlin at the time of the 'wall', at a time when some young people had just been killed trying to climb over this 'wall'. Butor in West Berlin was describing the atmosphere in a lecture room where he'd been speaking: how he was standing in the room, how the light from the projector lit up his hand, how he heard a noise, how he answered the questions, how his voice sounded, and so on. It was simply a literary exercise, of course, but at the same time it betrayed a profound contempt for the human drama, for the tragic events that were taking place at that very moment, a few hundred yards away from him: he was deliberately not noticing them.

Actually this disaffection is nothing new. It's not a characteristic of writers alone. Howath, a Hungarian writer, had already commented on it before the war. He was a teacher in an Austrian grammar school. He described how one day he'd seen four or five children hurling themselves at another boy and beating him up. He intervened, separated them, and said: 'Aren't you ashamed of yourselves, fighting four against one?' Whereupon the four or five boys, who probably joined the S.S. a few years later, looked quite expressionlessly at him, no feeling, no humanity in their eyes, their fish eyes. Well, it seems to me that more and more of us are getting like that. Of course I know that excessive guilt is a mistake, that it's paralysing; but the absence of guilt, or desolidarization in other words, is worse. It's a failing not just of the heart but of the intelligence. I accuse the new literature of the mandarins of lacking in intelligence, for all its clever tricks. This doesn't mean that there aren't some interesting experiments within the *nouveau roman*. There's Robert Pinget, Nathalie Sarraute, and possibly Claude Simon. They are writers. The others are just 'men of letters', emptied of all human substance: they are inhabited by an enormous vanity.

C.B. When you were talking about the cruel children, you talked about fish eyes, an empty gaze. But the gaze of Robbe-Grillet seems to me on the contrary to be an acute gaze which, though it doesn't attempt to get to the heart of a character's feelings, since it's equally true that one can never put oneself in someone else's place, does at least observe the most minute details of facts and behaviour and lay them bare.

154

E.I. But the article of Butor's I was mentioning proves exactly the opposite. Obviously, looking, trying to understand what one sees, to decipher people's behaviour from the outside, *can* be done in literature. Everybody can do it, and Simenon already has. In one of his novels, a teacher witnesses a crime taking place on the opposite side of the street. Since he has seen the crime and is so full of it that, emotionally, it's as though he'd taken part in it —albeit without interfering—he ends up being arrested. His moral guilt becomes a kind of material guilt and one ends up no longer knowing whether he simply witnessed the crime or actually committed it.

C.B. So you don't think the *nouveau roman* could constitute an important addition to contemporary literature?

E.I. I think it's a specifically French phenomenon, in the parochial sense, and that this phenomenon leads to a dead-end. I also think that later on people will laugh at these novels, these works. Take *Last Year in Marienbad* by Robbe-Grillet and Resnais. I'm only too happy to believe Robbe-Grillet when he says he's largely responsible for this film, because Resnais, who made *Night and Fog*, is far more noble, more generous, more free, more alive. I think that in a few years from now people will laugh immoderately at the characters in this film. They'll laugh because the characters are empty. You have the feeling that with every shot the scriptwriter is trying to say to us: 'Look how intelligent I am, look how original I can be.' When in fact there's nothing there, nothing but characters with unseeing eyes, like tailor's dummies.

C.B. But isn't the film trying to show a vain and empty society, to show it from the outside without any attempt at explanation?

E.I. People are the same in all societies, the people in this film are a reflection of the inner emptiness of its author.

There's no criticism in it of a spiritual void in other people, but rather an inability to know them, an indifference towards them, an inability to see beyond the surface.

C.B. Doesn't the château in Marienbad belong to the world of *Vogue* magazine? Hasn't the *nouveau roman* freed the novel of psychology in the same way you freed the theatre in *The Bald Prima Donna*?

E.I. It seems to me that I wanted my plays to contain a denunciation of mechanization and emptiness. One can escape from total emptiness, from total void, if this denunciation is tragic. And anyway there's a questioning, at least I hope there is; and if my characters are puppets, they're unhappy puppets. Caricature is a form of criticism. My characters are ludicrous because they're nothing. But in *Marienbad*, the characters are solemn and unfamiliar.

C.B. Is your real complaint against the *nouveau roman* that it's eliminated the tragic dimension?

E.I. Exactly. I don't know whether my plays work or not, but I've tried to show characters who are seeking a kind of life, an essential reality. They suffer at being cut off from themselves. That's what absurdity is, people being cut off from their roots, seeking desperately for themselves in the same way that in Kafka—whose principal theme is the labyrinth—the characters are seeking their own deep reality. And these characters suffer from not being, they suffer from their lack, whereas in a certain kind of literature they no longer even suffer from it. They've been dehumanized.

C.B. Do you think that contemporary literature is going through a crisis, that it will have to find new lines to work on?

E.I.   Thank heavens there *is* a crisis. I'd be really frightened if we no longer had crises. If there's a crisis, it means there's a quest. We are constantly in a state of crisis. The whole of history is one long succession of crises. Nothing is definitive. There's no such thing as a classical era that can be filed away once and for all. Every age is transitional in relation to another age which is itself transitional. As long as there is crisis, as long as there is anguish, there is real life, cultural life, spiritual life. But the moment literature becomes academic, when writers become mandarins, when literature looks at itself and no longer looks at the world around it, then things rigidify, then there is death. Of course, nowadays, there's a whole branch of literature which has eyes for nothing but its own technique. It's just a kind of tinkering.

C.B.   What importance do you personally attach to technique?

E.I.   One can't not be interested in technique. A writer can't not be interested in his means of expression, and in a sense the history of any art is the history of its means of expression. Only you should first of all be interested in what you have to say, then in the means that enable you to express it, and not first of all in technique. Actually, the quest for form and the quest for content should mean the same thing because everything is both form and content simultaneously. In art, you are trying to translate certain incommunicable things, incommunicable not because they cannot basically be communicated but because they have not yet been expressed. When you think about it, things are incommunicable in the beginning because they have not yet been communicated, and incommunicable in the end because the expressions that prop them up have been worn out. I personally am trying to express certain inner realities: images that suddenly loom up. Of course I'm interested in how I express them, in the same way that right now I'm trying to find the words to answer your questions, but I don't consciously select every word.

C.B. So ideally technique is something you can just forget about?

E.I. Of course, though even that is being too preoccupied with technique. In any case, in the *nouveau roman* you often have nothing but a description of surfaces: the soul is wiped out.

C.B. We were just talking about the crisis in literature. But there's also a lot of talk about the crisis in the theatre. Do you think these two crises are connected?

E.I. The crisis in the theatre is a crisis about renewing the means of expression. I'm contradicting what I was saying earlier on. It's a question of finding the words to say the things which have not yet been entirely said or which have been said in a different way. Apart from this—which is essentially a literary problem—the theatre has a specific crisis of its own. One could even say several crises. First of all there's the kindergarten mentality of the theatre people, who want to teach instead of discovering things together, with the audience. (And who anyway need first to think things out for themselves.) But perhaps they don't possess the necessary means for this discovery. There's also the fact that the public is used to going to the theatre to see realistic works. Whereas it accepts non-realism in the other arts, it won't accept it in the theatre. We've already discussed this: the public finds it hard to understand that the fantastic can be created other than by the use of machinery, but at the same time, it doesn't like machinery. The public has still to be initiated.

C.B. Don't you think drama centres and cultural centres can contribute to this initiation?

E.I.   If they were run by open-minded people. But not by
politicians or by the little old ladies who sponsor Christian
youth clubs. Let's hope that the people running these
theatres—even though they are intellectually and peda-
gogically inadequate—will manage to stimulate a movement among the young people.

C.B.   It seems to me that Planchon has already introduced an
interesting theatrical style. And at least he's given the inhabitants of Villeurbanne a chance to get to know the
major classics.

E.I.   I've seen very little of his work, but I don't like the idea of
rewriting Shakespeare and Molière, of sticking arms on
the Venus de Milo. You have the right to give several
interpretations of an author, to show his work in a new
light, but not to distort the sense of his work to provide
grist for your own ideological mill.

C.B.   Personally, I was delighted with Planchon's interpretation of *George Dandin*. He managed to establish life on
the farm as something real, and to show Dandin caught
between the peasants whom he's always lived with and
his in-laws who are rich bourgeois. He may have started
from a Marxist analysis, but this enabled him to create a
production that was very much alive.

E.I.   The real bourgeois was Dandin. And if he's punished, it's
because he was too much in love with the aristocracy,
because he wanted an aristocratic wife. He didn't have
enough self respect. If he's punished, he deserved to be.
Perhaps that's the real moral of the play.

C.B.   What do you regard as the right way for a modern producer to approach one of the classics?

E.I.   Well, for a start you don't distort it; you don't rewrite
history the way Stalin's scribes and some of the post-

Stalinists did; of course it's all right to have a different interpretation, provided you don't *change* the object; you don't put a moustache on the Mona Lisa and then tell the people you invite to see it: 'You see, we've demystified the Mona Lisa; she always did have a moustache but it was hidden from you.' Similarly, you don't change a noble duel into a cowardly murder, the way Planchon did in the Shakespeare play because he wanted to 'demystify chivalry': because Shakespeare *didn't* want to demystify chivalry, and besides, when he wanted to, Shakespeare didn't hesitate to paint extremely gloomy portraits of his princes.

Claude Bonnefoy. Since 1950, there's been a lot of talk about the *avant-garde* theatre. What does this expression mean to you? How important do you think this theatre is? Which playwrights do you find most interesting?

Eugène Ionesco. I don't know exactly what *avant-garde* theatre is. But I can say that there's a type of theatre, right now, which is introducing a new form of expression. It seems to me that what's happening now in the theatre is what happened in literature in the nineteenth century. First of all there were the Romantics—Musset, Lamartine—speechifying about sadness, melancholy, despair; then there was a real deepening with Lautréamont and Rimbaud who no longer spoke of despair and sadness but who lived their sadness and their despair. With them, literature went beyond reasoned speeches, there were no more reasoned speeches. Everything became an image, life, life even in the visceral sense. Nowadays we have good theatrical writers like Maulnier and Sartre who set out problems which their characters to some extent illustrate. But their plays are still full of reasoned speeches. In the plays of Weingarten and Dubillard on the other hand, the theatre has become visual, become imagery, anguish in concrete form. It's become as it is in the works of Boris Vian (I'm thinking of *Les Bâtisseurs d'Empire*) a living image and not a speech about uncertain truths.

C.B. What exactly do you mean by 'imagery' in the case of Dubillard, for example?

E.I. Well, perhaps, strictly speaking, what you find in Dubillard is sometimes not so much unusual images as an absence of speech, a certain song, a melancholy, characters torn between two worlds and living beyond words; the words state nothing, they merely suggest. In fact, the writers of the new theatre are poets.

C.B. Wasn't this type of theatre already heralded by earlier generations of writers?

E.I. There were some attempts, but they didn't always succeed—too many preconceptions, too cerebral. There were the efforts of certain surrealists, Philippe Soupault, possibly Desnos, possibly Tzara, possibly Picasso (*Desire Caught by the Tail*), possibly Vitrac. And most important, there was Jarry. *Ubu Roi* is a sensational play in which he doesn't talk about tyranny, he *shows* it in the form of that odious clown, Père Ubu, who is the archetype of moral, political and material gluttony.

C.B. Which contemporary writer do you most admire?

E.I. I don't know. I like Dubillard, Weingarten, Amos Kenan. . . .

161

C.B. Obaldia?

E.I. No, at any rate not yet. Arrabal . . . he still lacks something, some force, some dimension. He'll find it, though. But three or four important authors, that's already a lot, isn't it?

C.B. What about Beckett?

E.I. I really like what he's done, of course, even though he has become too systematic. He's cleared the stage of its accessories, he's made no concessions to the audience, he knows how to write and knows how to think, only his plays seem to be moving towards gimmickry. It's as if *now* he was making concessions to *his* audience, the audience he formed. You sometimes get the feeling he's no longer trying to say what he has to say, but to find gimmicks that will leave the audience gasping. After the dustbins, it was the basins, then he buried his characters, and so on. It's a permanent succession of daring feats.

C.B. It seems to me that he's less interested in daring than in purification, bareness, silence. . . .

E.I. Of course there's a basic sincerity. In his quest for new techniques, there's the expression of something he's trying to encompass or to reach. I have the feeling that, for the time being, he's becoming a formalist, not—obviously—in the sense that pedants or militants use the word. I think that right now he's most concerned with purely formal experiments, because he's already said the most important things he had to say, and said them several times, in *Waiting for Godot*, in *Endgame*, in *Happy Days!*

C.B. Do you think young dramatists should seek their inspiration in Beckett, or do you think that, after this attenuated theatre, they should look for something else?

E.I. In any case, Beckett's cultivating his disciples. I think he's one of the few living writers—apart from the *nouveau roman* people—who wants disciples, not so he can become the head of a literary school (with him it's more subtle, more human than with the new novelists), but so there can be a Beckettian family. Having disciples is dangerous because the school is always inferior to the master. At the same time, if there are no disciples, it may mean that the new form of stylistic expression isn't anchored in living reality. But these contradictions are inevitable in literature.

C.B. But doesn't a literary school demand that you take a position, for or against it, and doesn't it in this way pose the question of what should be done in the future?

E.I. That's what schools are good for: creating a style that will have to be destroyed.

C.B. Couldn't the *avant-garde* theatre at the present time be regarded as a school?

E.I. There's a difference between a current and a school. A current can't be created by one or two people, it takes ten, fifteen, twenty writers. When it reaches four hundred, it's all over.

C.B. You haven't mentioned Audiberti and Vauthier. Where would you place their plays, and how would you situate your plays in relation to theirs?

E.I. They both have a real mastery of language. Vauthier is possibly more dramatic, more theatrical, Audiberti is perhaps richer in verbal invention. In any event, they've restored to the theatre a verbal quality that the theatre seemed to have lost. Playwrights, particularly the *théâtre de boulevard* ones, have no sense of literary quality. Yet it's through literary quality that a work can survive.

163

I certainly don't have the verbal richness of Vauthier—still less of Audiberti— yet I have tried to create a different type of theatre and to find for it a poetic tone which doesn't exist in spoken language but only in the language of imagery. As far as spoken language is concerned, I tried in my first plays to make fun of it, to pull it apart. I did this as a reaction to a theatre that was not sufficiently poetic in its literary expression, and also because I was trying to strangle the phoney eloquence that one finds on the stage.

C.B.   In your most recent play, *Hunger and Thirst*, your concern with poetic language is far more marked than in your previous works.

E.I.   In *Hunger and Thirst*, as in *Exit the King*, the language is more literary in the classical, traditional sense, but when I say traditional I don't mean it's a return to the *théâtre de boulevard* tradition.

C.B.   Doesn't the *théâtre de boulevard* essentially reflect the tastes of the bourgeois society at the end of the nineteenth century, its tastes and its pastimes: salons, adultery, etc. . . ?

E.I.   Perhaps. A theatre that wasn't critical of them. In every society, there's a type of bad theatre that is popular with the public. There were countless farces in the Middle Ages. How many survived? In the nineteenth century, and it's even more clear-cut with the increase in writing, the fall-out was considerable. There are very few works that have really lasted. There's Hugo, and the elder Dumas, of course, but the theatrical quality of their works seems pretty thin to me. I can only find two authors in the nineteenth century whose works had any great theatrical quality. They're both at the end of the century: Claudel, with his explosive lyricism, and Jarry. In Jarry too you find the quest for a new type of language, a concise, caricatural, primitive language. His characters are extremely powerful, violent, rich, colourful and real. King Ubu is a character who transcends time: the critique of a certain human type, seen both in his time and in his permanence.

C.B.   Isn't this double theme of stupidity and tyranny that one finds in *Ubu Roi* very close to the themes of your own plays, particularly *Rhinoceros*?

E.I.   I hope so. Ubu is a character who's so simplified that he becomes an archetype, an incarnation of the power and truth of myth. He's dehumanized because he's so human, human in the worst and lowest ways. I was possibly influenced by him when I made monsters of my own characters, when I turned them into rhinoceroses.

C.B.   Your answers have suggested two questions to me. First: what is the relationship between poetry and plays?

E.I.   Plays are a form of poetry, just as poems are poetry, just as novels are poetry. Poetry means creation, etymologically. Where there's creation, there is poetry. The label 'poetic theatre' has often been applied to plays written according to certain rules or stylistic fashions that passed for poetic at particular times. But wherever you find the creation of a world and of characters, characters who are at once imaginary and real, there you have poetry.

C.B.   Secondly, since you used the word 'myth' in talking about Jarry, do you consider it the function of the theatre to represent the great myths of an age or the great myths of humanity?

E.I.   Definitely. Only it can't be done too consciously. If you're *trying* to create an archetypal character, you'll never manage it. Mythical reality can of course be analysed. It can't be understood lucidly. But it also comes from the uncontrollable and unconscious depths. If you are determined at all costs to demonstrate myths, instead of a mythical play, you will produce an intellectual or an ideological one. In fact, it's the public, the critics, posterity, who after a certain time, can discover the mythical value of a theatrical character.

C.B. When you read or see your plays again, do you ever think that one of your characters may become an archetype, that one day people may talk about Bérenger in the same way they talk about Orestes or Rodrigue?

E.I. That's every writer's ambition. But none of us can say we have succeeded. It isn't for me to judge my works and my characters. The only judgment I've passed has been on some of the realities in which they happened to find themselves. It was the situations that created them. If there is a mythical character, it probably won't be Bérenger, it will be the Rhinoceros. Anyway, I'll answer you one or two centuries from now, if I get the chance to re-read my works then . . . to become my own posterity. Most likely, it won't happen. It's very possible that *Rhinoceros* will become incomprehensible—I hope it will—in a world where all men have become lucid, with free personalities and autonomy of thought, and yet not separated from one another. When that world exists, people will no longer understand what I was trying to say. Or else they'll try to decipher my play like some document from a vanished era. I hope this will happen.

Claude Bonnefoy. Finally, Eugène Ionesco, what kind of future do you think is in store for literature?

Eugène Ionesco. I wonder if art hasn't reached a dead-end, if indeed in its present form, it hasn't already reached its end. Once, writers and poets were venerated as seers and prophets. They had a certain intuition, a sharper sensitivity than their contemporaries, better still, they discovered things and their imaginations went beyond the discoveries even of science itself, to things science would only establish twenty-five or fifty years later. In relation to the state of psychology in his time, Proust was a precursor.

But for some time now, science and the psychology of the subconscious have been making enormous progress, whereas the empirical revelations of writers have been making very little. In these conditions, can literature still be considered as a means to knowledge? Furthermore, in several countries, literature is prevented from being what it might still be. It no longer has the freedom to explore, it is required to illustrate dogmas and prejudices. Whereas at the time of its greatness, it denounced all prejudices, nowadays it is often compelled to justify them, to elaborate them and spread them. But in these same countries where literature is fettered, they can't stop science from making extraordinary leaps forward; and this is perhaps why science is moving increasingly ahead of literature.

People used to describe a landscape as looking like a painting, to say that some real situation resembed a situation they'd read about in a novel or seen in the theatre. But with space travel and the extraordinary vision that the cosmonauts have had, it's now literature that has to rise to the level of reality. No poet succeeded in suggesting or imagining or foreseeing the cosmic spectacle that the cosmonauts have seen.

Take television, and consider the plays and films you can see on TV. Telstar in itself is an amazing achievement.

But it's used to bring us a play by Terence Rattigan. Similarly, the cinema is more interesting as an achievement than the films that are shown in its theatres. The cinema and radio and television are miraculous things, whereas films and radio plays and television shows are no longer in the least surprising or miraculous. The ascent of the human mind is being expressed in technology, while art and literature lag increasingly behind the times.

C.B. Isn't there a danger that this pessimism will deter you from writing?

E.I. I'm a writer, I'm what you might call a professional, card-carrying artist. If I make such a despairing observation, it's in hopes of being contradicted or reassured. But I don't see, for the moment, that literature can give us more than it has already given. The *nouveau roman* is just a tinkering about. Calder too is just tinkering about. And Agnès Varda's films, even though she does think they're philosophy.

As for me, I want only to be what I am. What I should not have liked to be is a politician. It's heart-breaking that the world should still be ruled by politicians, when politics is even further behind science than literature is. For the humblest scientific researcher is infinitely more important than the highest head of State or any other celebrity.

C.B. If you are a writer and choose to remain one, isn't it because, in spite of everything, in spite of becoming aware of their own limitations, literature and poetry correspond by their very nature to a need that science will never be able to satisfy?

E.I. If literature still exists, perhaps it's because it does answer a need. To produce literature is to serve a function. The form in which literature is currently presented is inadequate. The imagination cannot not continue to function.

168

But it will be some time before the poet's imaginative function regains its former worth, before the poet has assimilated the world of technology which is, right now beyond him. For the moment, literature's field of exploration seems to me a closed one, literature can invent nothing but minor details. Out of Telstar, Rattigan and even Saint-John Perse, Telstar has to win every time.

C.B. I think your answer contains two important points: first, for a long time it was possible for the imagination to keep several steps ahead of knowledge, and literature, like science, was the instrument for investigation. But only science could bring certainty. Today, scientists have advanced their field so far that the writer can no longer keep ahead of it, and what naturally emerges from this is a gap between science—whose domain is knowledge and whose aims are objectivity and universality—and literature—whose domain appears increasingly to be that of curiosities, of feelings and emotions. Secondly— and this is accentuating the crisis of literature, and of art in general—the results of science (television, the exploration of space) give a reality to the incredible marvels imagined by Jules Verne and, long before him, Cyrano de Bergerac in *Les Etats de la Lune et du Soleil*.

But if science, more precisely the techniques that science gives rise to, seem for the moment to be beyond the writer's imagination, doesn't this explain why writers today are taking a serious look at themselves, asking themselves what literature is, trying to define its techniques? Ought we to see in this a secret desire on the part of the writer to be a technician as well, or just an attempt to define what literature specifically is?

E.I. As I said a few minutes ago, this technique is just tinkering. Writers want to imitate science, or to be inspired by it, to use its methods. They're wrong. If literature and poetry have any domain, it's the domain of feeling.

What I find annoying in the *nouveau roman* writers is that in their desire to be scientific they're destroying feeling. They're only very minor technicians, mere mechanics. But as long as we remain capable of emotion, people will continue to feel the necessity of art. Everything is passion, and passion alone. You could even say that if there were no passions, no desires, no nostalgia, there would be no science, either.

C.B. Is there no hope left for literature?

E.I. I hope this is just a temporary end, that literature—like the phoenix—will be reborn from its ashes. But it will look quite different. Right now, literature is dying; but it fulfils a function which will, I think, become clear again, in a new form. The novel is no longer possible. Poetry, even the poetry of Saint-John Perse, has become mere playing with words. The theatre is very often an inferior type of literature, by which I mean that the things that get presented on the stage are destined for people with inadequate imaginations. Anyone with sufficient imaginative resources doesn't need to go to the theatre. In fact, the theatre should be a ceremony, a ritual. But it's more often an instrument of propaganda.

C.B. What should the theatre be in our scientific world?

E.I. It should—materially—be an exploration, a concrete experience, it should enable us to imagine things better, it should be the unexpected. I'm thinking for instance of the new American theatre; of 'the happening' where suddenly people are on the stage and beginning not only to imagine, but to live out what they imagine, to create things and events which are as much of a surprise to them as they are to the audience. Ultimately, with the audience all participating, everyone should be an author. Formerly, authors proposed a mode of imaginative life. Now the art of the theatre must give to each person the possibility of living, of being a poet, of bringing out his own particular piece of the unforeseen.

C.B. Does this lead you to doubt your own activity as a dramatist?

E.I. In point of fact, I ought not to write any more plays. I write plays because I'm an author, just as anyone could be. There will, I hope, be more and more authors. When I write, it's a written improvisation which will later be repeated on a stage. Writing is my way of improvising. But I also have a moralist side to me. I want to denounce certain wrongs. This is not, perhaps, the function of art, which should be to make the unreal real, to raise up the unexpected. All the same, when you come right down to it, I do think there are still *some* little things to be done.

C.B. In fact, despite their surface contradictions, there is nothing incompatible about your two statements: literature is over, literature can still contribute something. In the future, science will offer us an understanding of the universe and of life, but literature will be the spontaneous manifestation of life, even life's natural reaction against all scientific or pseudo-scientific dogmatism. Is that what you meant?

E.I. Possibly. I must say in conclusion that we've talked a lot about humour: there's been very little of it in our conversations. Might this just possibly be a very tortuous way of being humorous?

Pataphysically speaking, gravity and solemnity are still forms of humour.

Ionesco
According to his
Contemporaries

OR

What the Critics Say

The Bald Prima Donna

This, its author explains, is an 'anti-play'. . . . And if it's immediately obvious that this definition is supposed to be provocative, it's less obvious what it's supposed to mean . . . however, after you've seen the play, you'll understand: it's the only intelligible phrase that Monsieur Ionesco has hit upon, with or without the help of his dictionary.

. . . . .

But one really must admire the superhuman courage of those who have so faultlessly remembered, interpreted, embodied and refined Monsieur Ionesco's anti-text. What wonders will they not perform when, lured on by the sweet smell of success and the heady perfume of pastures new, they discover either Molière or Vitrac?

Meanwhile, they are driving people out of the theatre. . . .

J. P. JEENER
Le Figaro, 13 May 1950

This is the most intelligently insolent play available to those who love the theatre more than directors do, who love wisdom more than professors do, who love better tragedy than that served up at the Grand Guignol and better farce than was ever seen at the Pont-Neuf. When we are old, we shall bask in the glory of having seen performances of *The Bald Prima Donna* and *The Lesson*.

JACQUES LEMARCHAND
Le Figaro Littéraire, October 1952

Jacques or Obedience—The Picture

Were he to put his undeniable gifts as a writer to serious use, he would produce works of importance. But *The Picture* and *Jacques*, which we have just seen, are peanuts for monkeys.

The dialogue, whatever one makes of it, is coarse. Not the best, as the butcher would say. It's mildly amusing; but as soon as we learn that the patron is penniless; when, with a pistol shot, he transforms his old hag of a sister into a raving beauty; when we read, in the words of Ionesco himself, that this farce is an ode to science, and to plastic surgery in particular, then there's nothing to do but give an amused shrug.

I marginally prefer *Jacques*, since its madness is undiluted by any serious pretensions.

ROBERT KEMP
Le Monde, 18 October 1955

There is nothing more dreary than an out-of-date joker.

Absurdity, foolishness, insanity, nonsense, stupidity as a dogma, spoonerisms, puns, shammed madness, laboured eccentricity, laborious originality, deliberate whimsy, souped-up extravagance, the ridiculous at all costs, the man who tickles himself to make us laugh, the man whose mission is to 'shake up the bourgeois', all this is very, very old hat. But never mind: the Huchette Theatre is small enough, and there are enough pretentious idiots in Paris, for these two works to find an audience.

JEAN-JACQUES GAUTIER
Le Figaro

Robert Postec directs with a faithfulness and imaginativeness that do real justice to Ionesco's art. As a result, there are a few moments of the performance which reach a quite remarkable peak of dramatic intensity: I am thinking in particular of that frighteningly ludicrous scene in which we see the family and in-laws sniffing at the fiancée, feeling her; as lewd and precise as the Normandy wedding guests who so inspired Flaubert.

JACQUES LEMARCHAND
Le Figaro Littéraire

(Ionesco) . . . is an unnatural writer in the strongest sense of the word.

The Picture begins with a long scene between two characters, a frightful fat financier and a starving painter. . . . A good start— I said to myself—but then everything collapsed, burst like a punctured tire, and we were plunged headlong into murky absurdity. The financier's sister, a sort of female tramp whom we'd thought was a victim-figure, turned out to be a frightful harpy who terrorizes the man we'd thought was her tyrant. He, however, does manage to strike her, and she promptly turns into a young girl, exactly like the one in the painter's picture. I shall say no more. I don't mind admitting that I don't understand the play, but I can also guarantee that no one else will understand it any better.

GABRIEL MARCEL
Les Nouvelles Littéraires, 3 November 1955

The Chairs—Jacques or Obedience

Ionesco's plays seem not to wear at all well. This is probably because he demands from his audience a constant complicity of smiles, bitterness, sadism, grimaces and snobisms that date extremely fast.

C. B.
Le Figaro

Like Job on his dunghill, Brutus in his tent, Tête d'Or on his rock, the mad old couple in *The Chairs* are fast becoming, for our half-century, the theatrical symbol of men's inability to understand their history.

BERTRAND POIROT-DELPECH
Le Monde

(II) The Killer and Rhinoceros

The Killer

Symbolism, see what harm you've wrought! You rob a lively and original dramatist of much of his fire and his charm. *The*

Killer is a very cumbersome play, too cumbersome for the light-weight truths it bears. And for the spectator, however well-disposed, it is a crushing ordeal.

ROBERT KEMP
Le Monde, March 1959

The Killer presents us once again with some of its author's pet tricks: the proliferation of objects, the recourse to magnification, the repetition of various effects. But Ionesco stands back a little from himself and his obsessions. The world of the nightmare, which has never been suggested so convincingly, at last allows one to glimpse the possibility of an awakened world. It is hardly surprising that the language, too, should have become more human.

ANDRÉ ALTER
Témoignage Chrétien, 13 March 1959

The Killer seems to me the most important of Ionesco's plays. Not because it is in three acts, and the longest, the most complete of his theatre, but because it deals with the most enormous subject there is, the one that contains all subjects: man in the presence of evil, fighting against evil—an evil which can take on any face, any form, even that of indifference, which is possibly the most demoralizing of all.

MARCELLE CAPRON
Combat, 2 March 1959

There is no point in trying to see in these plays a symbol of the times we live in.

RENÉE SAUREL
Les Temps Modernes, April 1959

What has just taken place at the Théâtre Récamier is the birth of a human type who should take his place in our language like a Panurge, a Don Quixote, a Pickwick, a Prudhomme, a Marius. . . . But Monsieur Bérenger is above all a man of our time. He is a part of contemporary history, our history, and he resembles many people we know and whom we may well be wrong to make fun of and have no time for.

ELSA TRIOLET

Les Lettres Françaises, 5 March 1959

Ionesco has not only invented a form of theatre in which character, language, settings and props have gained a new function. He has also invented a new audience.

JEAN SELZ

Les Lettres Nouvelles, 4 March 1959

Rhinoceros

'I will not give in,' shouts the hero of *Rhinoceros* as he faces the temptations of conformity. Unfortunately, his author has already done so. . . . Let me make myself quite clear, it was right and proper that all Paris, like the rest of Europe, should have honoured the true poet, the Ionesco of *The Bald Prima Donna.* But an early convert still has the right to deplore the fact that after his brilliant discovery of the strangeness of banality, Ionesco should have fallen, en route, into the banality of strangeness and into the sermonizing symbolism he so vehemently denounced.

BERTRAND POIROT-DELPECH

Le Monde

Has Ionesco given up his original points of view, has he rallied to the call of committed art? Not at all: the meaning of this play is not connected with any specific political situation. It is not a guided missile, a military weapon: just as *The Killer* depicted the absurdity of the social order and took man's inability to face his destiny as its real target, so *Rhinoceros* leads to the rejection of all systems and ends with an image of man, standing upright and alone. There is throughout the same anguish and the same distress, but here, for the first time, there is also the affirmation that man's nobility consists in the fact that he has it in him to rebel.

ROBERT ABIRACHED

Etudes, 1960

Eugène Ionesco once brought something new to the contemporary French theatre: a criticism of conventional life and language, a particular vision of man's alienation in present-day society, a new and exciting dramatic style. His one-act plays were fully loaded and struck home. His three-act plays (*Rhinoceros, The Killer*) are duds and 'hang fire' (as they say in the artillery).

GUY LECLERC
L'Humanité

This time, no mistake about it, Ionesco is writing in French! And his *Rhinoceros* is a completely clear work, with its own limpid symbolism, all the more powerful for being accessible and all the greater because everyone can grasp its meaning.

JEAN VIGNERON
La Croix, February 1960

The first articles on the subject left me completely dumbfounded. Was I seeing straight? Had left-wing critics been infected by chronic rhinoceritis? How did it all begin? Had some invisible rhinoceroses contaminated the men-critics? Here they were rising like a unanimous rhinoceros against the play, judging it from the rhinoceros' point of view. . . . So as not to be caught off their guard, not to be left outside the clique of subtle rhinoceros-experts. Some even go so far as to take offence at the anti-Nazi satire, recognizing themselves in a portrayal which only our worst enemies would make of us. To shoot oneself in the back in this way is indeed the height of dexterity.

ELSA TRIOLET
Les Lettres Françaises, February 1960

Something very strange and amusing is going to take place, and indeed is already beginning to take place, in the attitude of the denigrators of Eugène Ionesco's plays. After shrugging their shoulders at plays whose success is now world-wide, though not necessarily popular for all that, dubbing them obscure, meaningless and in short real theatrical booby-traps, they are now going to declare them banal and commercial but still meaningless.

Then in the time-honoured fashion they will go on to flatten the new work by referring to the earlier ones, which they jeered at in their time. 'Oh, dear! What has happened to the Ionesco of *The Chairs*, of *How to Get Rid of It*? How has the extraordinary author of *The Bald Prima Donna* come to write a laboured farce like *Rhinoceros*?' This is what we shall hear, and we simply must not listen to it. What would we not have heard if Eugène Ionesco had persisted (and it would not have been difficult for him) in constantly rewriting *The Chairs*?

JACQUES LEMARCHAND
Le Figaro Littéraire, 30 January 1960

Ionesco reminds me of a man walking through a foreign capital looking for something he has lost. Those who know his plays know quite well that Ionesco no longer knows what it is exactly that he's looking for, nor even if he ever lost it. But he continues to look for it, to lose himself and to find himself again. His theatre is the account of this search, which is possibly pointless. But who knows?

GUY DUMUR
Arts, January 1960

London has given a cool reception to *Rhinoceros*, Eugène Ionesco's play, first performed in Paris by the Renaud-Barrault company.

France-Soir, 30 April 1960

The combination Ionesco - Sir Lawrence Olivier - Orson Welles triumphed on Thursday night with *Rhinoceros*, which the Royal Court, a kind of London Theatre Workshop, was presenting to the London public for the first time.

HENRI PIERRE
Le Monde, 30 April 1960

to be continued . . .

LIST OF WORKS AVAILABLE IN ENGLISH

PROSE

FRAGMENTS OF A JOURNAL
NOTES AND COUNTER NOTES

PLAYS

THREE PLAYS (*Amédée* or *How to get rid of it, The New Tenant, Victims of Duty*), translated by Donald Watson, 1958.

The Killer, Improvisation or *The Shepherd's Chameleon, Maid to Marry*, translated by Donald Watson, 1959.

Rhinoceros, The Leader, The Future Is in Eggs, translated by Derek Prouse, 1960.

Exit the King, translated by Donald Watson, 1967.

FOUR PLAYS (*The Bald Soprano, The Lesson, The Chairs, Jack, or the Submission*), translated by Donald Allen, 1968.

A Stroll in the Air, Frenzy for Two or More, translated by Donald Watson, 1969.

Hunger and Thirst, The Picture, Greetings, Anger, translated by Donald Watson, 1969.

Index of names

Index of titles